M000278186

GERMAN JERUSALEM

GERMAN JERUSALEM

The Remarkable Life of a German-Jewish Neighbourhood in the Holy City

THOMAS SPARR

First published in 2021 by
HAUS PUBLISHING LTD
4 Cinnamon Row
London SW11 3TW
www.hauspublishing.com

Copyright © Thomas Sparr, 2021

Translated from the German language: GRUNEWALD IM ORIENT
Das deutsch-jüdische Jerusalem
First published in Germany by Berenberg Verlag

English-language translation copyright © Stephen Brown, 2020
Excerpt from S. Y. Agnon, *Shira*, trans. Zeva Shapiro, © Toby Press, 2014
Excerpt from Lea Goldberg, *Selected Poetry and Drama*, trans. Rachel Tzvia Back,
© Toby Press, 2005

A CIP catalogue record for this book is available from the British Library

ISBN: 978-1-912208-61-6
eISBN: 978-1-912208-62-3

Typeset in Garamond by MacGuru Ltd

Printed in the United Kingdom by TJ Books

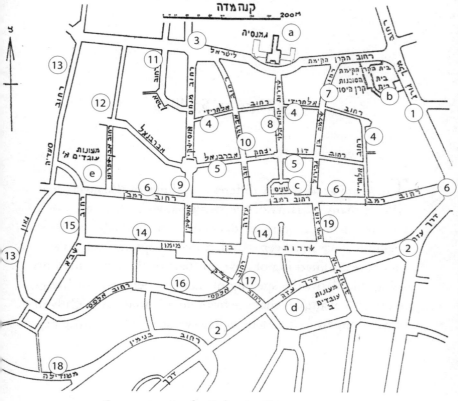

רחביה

קנה מדה

Street map in the Rehavia directory, 1936

1	King George Street	15	Rashba Street
2	Gaza Street	16	Alfasi Street
3	Keren Kayemet Le-Israel	17	Radak Street
4	Al-Harizi Street	18	Binyamin Mi-Tudela Street
5	Abarbanel Street	19	Arlozorov Street
6	Ramban Street		
7	Ibn Gabirol Street	a	The Hebrew Gymnasium
8	Yehuda ha-Levi Street	b	Offices of the KKL [Keren
9	Menahem Ussishkin Street		Kayemet Le-Israel: Jewish
10	Ibn Ezra Street		National Fund] and other
11	Haran Street		Jewish organisations
12	Ibn Shaprut Street	c	Tennis court
13	Saadia Gaon Street	d/e	Housing for manual and
14	Ben Maimon Boulevard		office workers

A Note on Spelling

There are at least four different spellings of 'Rehavia', likewise as many variants of the street names in the area, some German, some English or derived from the Hebrew. These spellings have not been standardised in quotations because they reveal something of how this part of the city came into being. Similarly, the spelling of names ('Bergman' or 'Bergmann', for example) changes from decade to decade. Only in transcribing from the Hebrew have we striven for consistency.

Contents

Foreword

When I arrived in Jerusalem in autumn 1986, to live and work there, I encountered a new world until then entirely unknown to me and yet oddly familiar. I plunged into it straightaway. It was as if I had been transported in a time machine. In the everyday life of the 'Yekkes', Jews from the German-speaking world, the men wearing jackets and ties, the women in their suits and dresses, I recognised the Weimar, Frankfurt, Berlin, Munich or Königsberg of the 1920s and 1930s. A past I had known only second-hand, from books and conversations, was now present before me, transplanted in space.

Thirty years ago, this past already lay a long way back; now it is more distant still. Scarcely any of the Yekkes who came to Israel from the Weimar Republic or Nazi Germany are alive today. But this distance, in paradoxical fashion, permits my description: what has vanished is more easily grasped than what is vanishing.

The world I want to describe in this book is concentrated in one neighbourhood of Jerusalem: Rehavia, Hebrew for 'the vastness of God'. A long stretch of time – from the decade and a half of the Weimar Republic, through the Nazi years 1933 to 1945 and into the post-war period – is gathered in a comparatively narrow space. This history extends over a handful of streets, squares, a few shops and cafés, in homes sparsely furnished with grand pianos and music stands, a few pictures and, above all, endless walls of books. Decades later these books would be cleared out to lie by the side of the road, tattered classics in old bindings: Goethe and Schiller, Kleist, Conrad Ferdinand Meyer and Gottfried Keller next to Zuckmayer's *The Devil's General*, single issues of *Die neue Rundschau*, a first edition of Thomas Mann's *Tonio Kröger*, works by Martin Buber or Heinrich Böll's *Billiards at Half-Past Nine* and Günter Grass's *Cat and Mouse*. The dishevelled stock of personal libraries, gathered and selected over years, ended up as bulk waste. The names and titles of the books in most cases meant as little to these Israeli grandchildren, great-nieces and nephews – the second generation had still understood at least some German – as the old furnishings, the heavy chests, tables and chairs. Back then I took for myself this or that specimen from those books carelessly abandoned at the roadside.

Rehavia was the 'German' – the German-Jewish – Jerusalem, capital of the Yekkes. They had come to that land by widely differing routes: fleeing, migrating, visiting, temporarily interned by the British mandatory powers, driven by Zionist self-determination or running from anti-Semitism and Nazi persecution, leaving their traumatised lives behind – which is to say, carrying their trauma with them. The testimonies that follow show this too.

Many of the immigrant Yekkes came from Berlin or had spent a significant part of their lives there. Rehavia incorporated something of the layout of the big city in its 'vastness of

God'. Residents and visitors alike called it the 'Grunewald of the East' after the genteel, bourgeois, leafy district in the west of Berlin, which had now been reborn, after a fashion, in West Jerusalem.

The inner geography of these few square kilometres is handed down to us in books, letters, pictures and photographs, in Else Lasker-Schüler's *Land of the Hebrews*, Gershom Scholem's autobiography *From Berlin to Jerusalem*, in the poems of Mascha Kaléko and the many letters she sent from Jerusalem, in the writings of Werner Kraft and others.

We begin in London, for many German Jews a significant stop on the way from Berlin to Jerusalem. Then, in Jerusalem, we see the protagonists of this book meeting rather fortuitously in a café in our part of the city. One evening at the beginning of the 1960s, six people seek and find each other. That they should have met like this is pure wishful thinking – and yet not just that. Their paths in Rehavia actually did cross, or we may presume they did. In the following chapters we trace out those paths and turning points, their locations, their particular origins in Berlin – that city remains the magnetic pole – and, above all, the intersections of Else Lasker-Schüler, Gershom Scholem, Werner Kraft, Mascha Kaléko, Anna Maria Jokl and others, each of them revealing a different aspect of this part of Jerusalem.

From the 1920s Rehavia became – to use Thomas Mann's phrase – a 'way of life and thought'. You could have found something kindred to it in Tel Aviv as well, in Haifa, on Mount Carmel or elsewhere in Israel, only without the particular density and shaping of a single neighbourhood.

The Hebrew University, some distance away on Mount

Scopus and later in neighbouring Givat Ram, was part of Rehavia; many students sublet rooms in the area. This Berlin-moulded neighbourhood had a small retail sector too: an ironmongers, hat shop, Meisler's Electrical Goods, clothes shops, news kiosks, bookshops, a cinema, the Café Atara, the Sichel and Rehavia coffeehouses and Käthe Dan's guesthouse, as well as daily German-language reading matter in *Blumenthals Neueste Nachrichten* ('Blumenthal's Latest News') – which became *Jedioth Chadashoth* ('Latest News' in Hebrew, printed in Roman script on the front page) and then *Israel-Nachrichten* or *Hadashoth Yisrael* ('Israel News' in both languages, this time with text in Hebrew as well as German) – and *MB*, the mostly German-language newsletter for German immigrants published in Tel Aviv.

Rehavia came into being on the drafting table of Richard Kauffmann, an architect from Germany who had immigrated in 1920 to develop plans for Hahsharat Ha-Yishuv, the Israel Land Development Company (previously the Palestine Land Development Company), which built residential areas and settlements for the Zionist movement.

The history of this city district may be told through its geography, architecture, urban planning or chronology. But the decisive thing is the biographies of its inhabitants, who moulded the history of the neighbourhood over decades, just as Rehavia shaped the paths of their lives. Within the individual biographies there are overlaps, synchronicities and delays – how could it be otherwise? – but all are held together by the grid map of the area.

Rehavia is laid out as a symmetrically ordered lattice of streets. But you couldn't draw an exact boundary around it with a ruler; it's more as if it's been outlined by the unsteady hand of a child. 'There are no clearly drawn borders between Talbiya, a mixed area, Rehavia, which was entirely Jewish, and the predominantly Arab Katamon,' writes Walter Laqueur in his portrait of the city.

You can give any number of different names to this neighbourhood's character, but each approaches the area and its essence only asymptotically. Taking the word 'Rehavia' literally will mislead you. The transport authorities have clogged up the 'vastness' that the urban planners envisaged. The fond nickname 'Grunewald of the East' emphasises the garden suburb aspect. David Kroyanker's handsome circumlocution 'a Prussian island in an Oriental sea' captures Rehavia's sense of isolation without entirely separating the island from the mainland of 'German' Jerusalem, the world of the German protestant Templers and settlers, of Kaiser Wilhelm II's visit to Jerusalem.

Else Lasker-Schüler's 'Dream City' properly means Thebes, that faraway city never to be found on this earth, which may be seen, at best, in silhouette. But with Lasker-Schüler, every dream carries within it the signature of the real. Every city in her life, be it Wuppertal, Berlin, Zürich or Jerusalem, absorbs particles of the others: 'My dreams fall into the world.' The dreamed city is reality in another state of matter. The literature of the dream city – in the writing of Lasker-Schüler as of S.Y. Agnon, Amos Oz and Yehuda Amichai – preserves, in its fixed layout, its floating dreams and its terrible nightmares, an exact memorial.

The Journey to London

Anna Maria Jokl set out in 1977 from Jerusalem to London. She had left London twenty-seven years earlier to move to Berlin – more precisely, to East Berlin, the capital of the then newly founded German Democratic Republic. Looking back, Jokl said that she had lived six lives, by which she meant her life had had six locations. She was born in Vienna on 23 January 1911 and would retain its inflections for her entire life. She moved to Berlin in 1928 after the death of her father, to be with her mother and her mother's new husband. There she worked through the last of the Roaring Twenties in theatre, radio and newspapers and was politically active as well, left-leaning. In 1933, being a Jewish woman, she fled Nazi Berlin for Prague – 'yes, the Czechs' – for whom all her life she retained a special affection. After six years in Prague, she set sail just in time for London via Danzig and its harbour city Gdynia, arriving on 1 May 1939. There she scraped a living working as a shorthand typist until, just over a decade later, she emigrated to East Berlin, from where she was expelled by the authorities, causing her to land up in West Berlin, where she worked as a psychotherapist at the Jewish Hospital before moving in 1965 into her sixth life – in Israel.

Six locations; six lives.

'To move from one house to another costs you a shirt; / From one place to another – a life.' Jokl put this Jewish proverb at the front of her book *The Journey to London*, her memoir recalling her years in the British capital and, frequently, her five other lives as well. Jokl was just twenty-two years old when she managed to flee from Berlin to Prague. She stayed there six years and wrote a book, *The Colour of Mother of Pearl*, which could not be published in German until years later.

In the story of German-Jewish emigration, Berlin, London and Jerusalem form a historical triangle. London stands in the middle – not geographically, but historically.

Gabriele Tergit made her way from Jerusalem to the British capital in 1938. This Berliner author, born Elise Hirschmann in 1894, the daughter of a German-Jewish family who grew up in the solidly middle-class Tiergarten area, made her name in the 1920s with her court reporting. As a young woman journalist, Tergit attended trials in the criminal courts in Moabit, a poor, proletarian district of Berlin. The testimonies of the accused – thieves, pimps, sex workers, petty criminals – and of the witnesses – caretakers, lower-middle-class people of all kinds – as well as the prosecutors' indictments and the judges' judgements gave in her articles a picture of Berlin society as graphic as the offences in question, the frauds and brazen muggings, murders and sex crimes. Even the guardians of order who intervened to stop them, the police, became unwitting chroniclers of their time. Using the pseudonym Gabriele Tergit and under the influence of Karl Kraus, she remade the genre of court reporting from simple reportage into the story of its time: of poor and rich, of the fault lines in society and the political tensions of the Weimar Republic.

Her novel *Käsebier Takes Berlin*, published in 1931, centres on the overnight celebrity of the singer Käsebier in Berlin's sensation-hungry newspapers in the winter of 1929. Eighty-five years after its original publication, Tergit's novel had a glittering comeback, finding a new audience by offering a slice of *Babylon Berlin* (the hit TV series about Weimar Berlin, broadcast from 2017). In November 1933 Tergit and her husband, the architect Heinz Reifenberg, emigrated to Jerusalem, where she became a chronicler of her new city and country.

In 1938 she moved finally to London, where she lived until her death in 1982. Thus a piece of Berlin made its way to the Thames, as she recalls in her memoir *Definitely Somewhat Unusual*:

> In the summer of 1946 I met a woman from St Petersburg who had come to London via Berlin and German philosophy. In a room as wretched as the most wretched of emigrée rooms she had conducted a 'salon' at which Monty Jacobs, features editor of the *Vossische Zeitung*, and Professor Hermann Friedmann met and founded Club 43, which exists still. The Club held lectures in German by well-known personalities, even as the German 'wonder weapons' the V1 and V2 were falling, and thus offered respite, stimulus and relaxation to hundreds, for next to no charge.

German emigrants who had landed up in London met at Club 43 pretty much every Monday evening from its founding in 1943. They listened to lectures and discussed the world situation, almost always in German – and this in the middle of the Second World War. We do not know whether the paths of Gabriele Tergit and Anna Maria Jokl crossed there at some point in the 1940s, nor whether they met each other later in Berlin, where Tergit travelled back to many times. From 1945 to 1949 Tergit wrote 'Letters from London' for the newly founded *Tagesspiegel* newspaper, reporting from the city that for her had become home. And yet the fixed point in her thinking and her feelings remained Berlin.

It was the same for Erich Mendelsohn, who after 1933 designed buildings in both London and Jerusalem, and carried on his Berlin work from both cities. He co-designed the Bexhill Pavilion on the Sussex coast. Later he decided to move entirely to Jerusalem, and took possession of Rehavia's windmill, the district's landmark, the first thing you see as you enter Rehavia. In the narrow spaces of the windmill Mendelsohn set up his studio and a flat.

It was there in 1935 that another Berliner, the young architect Julius Posener, met him. For Posener, too, London would later become an important staging post. Decades later, back in Berlin, Posener would recall his encounter with Mendelsohn in Rehavia. The two had quarrelled until Mendelsohn repaired the situation by putting one of Beethoven's late string quartets onto the record player:

> You may imagine the scene: two German Jews, one an artist and one who wants to become one, are sitting in a windmill in Jerusalem and listening to late Beethoven: the *Song of Thanksgiving* and the quartet that surrounds the *Song of Thanksgiving*. The players are – naturally – the Busch Quartet. The two men are listening to this "song" because

there has been a little skirmish between them and because in the light of the *Song of Thanksgiving* it counts for nothing – not for this pair. This was not simply a piece of beautiful music – Schubert's 'Symphony in B minor' would not have worked. Late Beethoven was the discovery of our time, towards which even our parents were a little sceptical. We had become proficient in it, just as we had become proficient in Bach. To us, Beethoven was of the greatest – and the closest – significance. We are in Palestine and we are pondering how we, two Jews in this land where we have our origins, can, may, should now build after the Arabs, who have inhabited this land for around a thousand years, have built on it so compellingly in their own way.

Posener left Israel for London in 1948 and taught at the Brixton School of Building. Eight years later he went with his family from there to Kuala Lumpur to teach. Five years after that he was faced with the choice of going back to Israel or returning after a quarter century to Berlin. He chose to return home and became a renowned historian of architecture in Germany.

Anna Maria Jokl travelled back to London in 1977 and in the middle of her stay in the city went to observe Yom Kippur in Bayswater, where she had previously lived for years. She made her way to the bus stop on Bayswater Road by a familiar route:

It was gloomy with an overcast sky as now, after twenty-seven years, I walked past the park railings into Kensington Gardens. There spread the broad lawns, there stood the tall trees, growing in their places as if by chance, though they had once been planted and left to stand there with the unerring instinct of the English gardener. Between the lawns you can see for hundreds of metres the yellowish sandy paths leading into the expanse of the park in three distinct diagonals. I knew them all, every metre imbued with thoughts and associations, experiences in spring, summer, autumn and even winter over many years. The park had been an oasis in what had remained for me an essentially foreign city; the prospects suddenly opening up and suddenly changing, the liberating broad swathe with the memorial at its end and the sky behind it, and then the trees, mighty and broadly spread, as no other country's are, in London's notorious wet; in each one you can still discern the spiral's principle of growth, which thickens in yearly rings from the germ onwards at a vegetable pace.

The tree I was looking for had stood near the entrance in the middle of an area of grass. In all these years I had not forgotten it.

In 1944 Jokl had been assigned the job of air raid warden in the Civil Defence Service for a boarding house. One spring night German aircraft attacked. She waited it out with the guests in the basement, listening as the bombs hit nearby. When Jokl walked out of the house the following morning, she saw that the crown of one of the tall, broadly spread trees had been torn to shreds. Leaves and shattered branches were strewn across a wide area. Jokl condenses into a single image what is ostensibly an episode from the Second World War but in reality stands for its entire epoch:

Less than a metre remained of that mighty trunk. Its pale insides were split open like some vast wound of sharp wood fibres. From such splendour, this was what remained. But by the autumn unnaturally large leaves, ten times as large as normal leaves, had sprouted from the gaping wound in the tree; the life force of its mighty roots was thrust into those leaves. And in the following spring, thin twigs, poignantly out of proportion, grew out of the shredded stump, and in the six years I remained in London, the tree that had been struck little by little acquired a bizarre shape: a thin-branched crown of uncommonly youthful green sat enthroned on a low, wide trunk, as in a child's drawing. It was poignant and frightening at the same time, the way the tree had withstood that deadly blow, whose origin had nothing to do with its own being, and in doing so had taken on a bizarre and yet unmistakeable form.

In Kensington Gardens in 1977 Jokl set out in search of this tree and remembered how she once met B., an officer in the Polish Army in exile – an unfulfilled lovers' encounter in an 'age of irreversible separations', as Jokl put it. B. returned to Warsaw and remained untraceable over the ensuing years. By the time the two revived their connection many years later, it was too late. 'Life does not simply stop. He had married and belatedly had a son – both knew of me and respected me. He wanted to come – I wrote, no. The moment of impossible decision had irretrievably passed.'

In *The Journey to London* Jokl takes her readers to all the locations of her life – Vienna, Berlin, Prague, London, East and West Berlin and Jerusalem – while she goes on a long walk through Kensington Gardens, searching: 'I had come to search for the tree, on Yom Kippur in London. I could no longer find it.'

In the 1980s Jokl wrote about her fifteen years living in Rehavia:

Here I sit at my typewriter in Jerusalem and look out over the bare Judaean Hills. Directly behind them the full moon rises, the moon to which we flew already some years ago. And I can still remember exactly the spot in the bay window where I heard on the crystal radio the unimaginable news that Lindbergh had become the first to fly across the ocean. I was fourteen years old then – and my diary for tomorrow is full with work, errands, a visit from a friend from life No. 4, from London during World War 2, and at noon a circumcision celebration for little Yakir, who will perhaps live into the middle of the 21st century, and in the evening a concert with Rubinstein, born 1890. How long does a life really last?

We forget nothing, as Anna Maria Jokl once wrote. We are everything that has happened, the fusion of every sequence of events into a simultaneous present, a new chemical element.

Alongside her mother tongue, Jokl had to learn three languages in her six lives: Czech, English and Hebrew. 'Whoever changes his country often, loses his life' – Jokl modifies this saying from the Midrash, and then interrupts herself: 'You lose. You gain. Who has a choice? 3 times I had none; the 4th migration was desired, certainly, but only the leaving, not the destination. Only Jerusalem I chose.'

Jokl moved to Rehavia. Martin Buber, whom she had sought out and connected with on her first trip to Israel, died in the year of her arrival, 1965. She became friends with Escha and Shmuel Hugo Bergmann and joined herself to a new circle in Jerusalem while maintaining her connections to those from her earlier lives. Yet her last book, *From Six Lives* (2011), edited from her papers after her death by Jennifer Tharr, also shows how the changes in her life ruptured her loving relationships.

Her first Hebrew publication after she immigrated was *Two Cases on the Theme 'Overcoming the Past'*, cases she had brought with her from Germany and with which she gave new impetus to Israeli analysts and therapists. Around 1960 in West Berlin, a young Jew, Yehuda, and a German, Volker, both around twenty-five years old, had consulted her, neither knowing anything of the other. Both suffered agonies both physical and mental. Yehuda had survived two years in a cave in Poland after escaping from the ghetto. Volker had been raised in a National Socialist boarding school. Their separate paths through life meet in their terrible dreams of destruction and violence. In her lucid prose Jokl reveals the convergences, the similar disturbances of two so divided. It is one of the earliest and at the same time most compelling psychoanalytic contributions to German-Jewish history.

I met Jokl in 1987 in the library of the Leo Baeck Institute in Jerusalem, which researches the history of the Jews from Germany. Her sceptical friendly gaze met mine, and I was curious. Jokl gave me an old book, for children, published in 1948 by Dietz Verlag in East Berlin: *The Colour of Mother of Pearl*. She had written it in 1937 in Prague. This 'Children's

Book for Almost Everyone' is a parable of the dawning world of Nazism. It tells of the conflict between two school classes, of an autocratic ringleader, of submissiveness, betrayal and the longing for a 'strongman' in a school in Berlin in the 1920s – or is it not also a school in Haifa, Ramallah, Paris, Peking, Washington or Moscow? Wolfgang Staudte prepared a film version of *The Colour of Mother of Pearl* – in 1950 one of the best-selling children's books – for DEFA (the state-owned film studio in East Germany), but the East German authorities banned it. When Siegfried Unseld republished the book in 1992, it became a success and was translated into other languages. Its language and its content were clear, timeless.

In her old age Jokl still seemed peculiarly young. She was resolute and could be curtly dismissive. Throughout her six lives she had remained reliant on herself, in her first apprenticeship as a nursery teacher, after she received her school-leaving certificate, then later as an actress, with her work for radio, as a director, as a shorthand typist in exile, as an author and later still as a psychotherapist, following a training analysis with Toni Sussmann and a long confrontation with Carl Jung. The natural sciences interested her, as did the prime numbers, about which she wrote a children's book in Prague called *The True Wonders of Basilius Knox*. With the revival of Hebrew in Jewish daily life, she was especially intrigued by the system of instruction developed by her teacher Mordechai Kamrat. She was no stranger to Hasidism or mysticism either.

Jokl had by nature a particular brevity, a tightening, a turn to the fundamental. Her prose pieces, collected as *Essences*, condense entire epochs into vignettes and portraits: a waltz on the evening before the outbreak of war in Prague; an encounter at the Dead Sea; the figure of old Jan, searching for his lost roots in Poland; the playwright Ödön von Horváth; the duration of a cigarette in Tel Aviv; and a stone on an unknown grave – the grave of Kafka's sister Ottla. How casually an incident or image makes an entire world of connections visible.

Jokl's mother and stepfather were deported from Berlin to Riga on 25 January 1942. Their dates of death are unknown. Every year on her mother's birthday, 5 May, Jokl asked herself whether the lilacs were already in bloom. She describes how, on the first 5 May after she returned to post-war Berlin, she threw a bunch of lilacs into her parents' bombed-out home in Berlin's Tiergarten. We are everything that has happened.

Evening in Jerusalem

The day was already dimming, and the entire earth changed its aspect. The streets suppressed their tumult, some roads turning white, others graying. The air close to the ground became black; closer to the sky, it was pink; and the air in between was nondescript, colorless. The trees on [Ben] Maimon Boulevard, along with the men and women who strolled by, were engrossed in a secret they themselves were unaware of. Some of these strollers seemed to be saying: You don't realize who we are.

S.Y. Agnon, *Shira*

Late afternoon in Rehavia on a Saturday at the beginning of the 1960s. Shabbat silence covers the vastness of God. In the afternoon of Shabbat the streets are even quieter. Not until the evening, Motza'ei Shabbat, does the life flow back into the veins of the city and Rehavia grow livelier, noisier. Buses and cars drive past, people listen to music and news bulletins on the radio, cinemas and theatres open their doors. At around half past eight the concerts begin. With its Bauhaus style, unmistakeable sand-coloured Jerusalem stone and narrow streets, with its frequent sounds of piano-playing, its trees – eucalyptus, pine, palm and jacaranda – and its meticulously trimmed box hedges, Rehavia has the look of a suburb.

To its residents from Berlin, it might seem like leafy Dahlem, but Rehavia isn't a suburb at all: it lies close to the centre of West Jerusalem, not far from Jaffa Street and Ben Yehuda Street, Zion Square and the Jewish market at Mahane Yehuda. The Old City is just a few kilometres away, but at the beginning of the 1960s the way is still blocked by fences, walls and barbed wire. Jerusalem's historic Old City belongs to Jordan. A border has separated West and East Jerusalem since 1948. There are frequent gun battles along it. From the edge of Rehavia you can hear the shots and see the fires.

The German-language newspaper *Jedioth Chadaschoth* announces a piano concert 'at Shabbat's end, around 8.30pm'. Daniel Barenboim is playing Mozart sonatas. One advertisement offers 'Popular Excursions from Tel Aviv, Haifa and Jerusalem to Eilat [the new city on the Red Sea] on two days – Wednesday and Friday' or 'Sodom on one day – Thursday' and promises 'Popular Prices / Explanations in the usual languages', which certainly include German. Another advert addresses itself to 'Restitution Recipients': 'We deliver world-renowned premium brand-name goods to you for your 33% from the Compensation Funds, including Grundig hi-fi equipment … Zeiss Ikon optical equipment. Don't be fooled. Check carefully for our company name.' On 16 February 1961 the rainfall for 'this year's rainy season' is measured at 335.6 millimetres. 'The capital city was gripped by bitter cold in the early hours of yesterday morning.' And at the beginning of the 1960s Robert Stolz, by then over eighty years old, is conducting the Israel Philharmonic Orchestra, offering 'A Night in Vienna' not far from this part of the city, at the vast concert hall of Binyenei Ha'Uma.

On this Shabbat evening Gershom Scholem leaves his home on Abarbanel Street and walks to the corner of King George Street before turning left. He is sunk in thought. Scholem is no café-goer; his Prussian temperament revolts at the thought of a café and all that goes with it – the expansive study of newspapers, the hours of loitering, the random table talk, the squandered time. Today, however, he is making an exception and meeting with Martin Buber, whose origins are in Austria-Hungary and who lived and studied for years in Vienna. Generally the older man – Buber is eighty-three – receives guests at his house. But Buber's home in Talbiya, a neighbourhood adjoining Rehavia, would be the wrong location for this Saturday's appointment. It was there, at Buber's house, a few weeks earlier, that friends and kindred spirits, professors and publishers presented to Buber the final volume of his translation of the Bible, which he had begun, in collaboration with Franz Rosenzweig, nearly forty years before.

'Our dear Herr Buber,' Scholem had said, 'as we have gathered today in your house to celebrate the noteworthy day of completion of your Bible translation into German, something akin to the old Jewish "siyum" to mark the completion of a course of study, so is this for us a notable opportunity to reflect on your work, its purpose and its achievement.' And it was precisely this address, which ought to have been an encomium, that had brought into the open a disagreement between Scholem and Buber, not a new dispute, but one which here broke out in force. Their conflict touched on everything: the traditions handed down within Judaism, the manner in which they should be read, the conclusions the two drew from them. On the surface it was just two scholars disputing between themselves. But it was not that. At its heart their disagreement concerned the relationship between Germans and Jews; its historical burden; the two peoples' dealings with each other; the possibility of rapprochement between them; and the relationship of two states, Germany and Israel. It is not by chance but rather testament to a whole network of historical relationships that this controversy was ignited by a translation of the Bible – and that it was happening at the beginning of the 1960s in one place in the world: Rehavia.

This evening in Café Atara, sitting next to Buber, is Anna Maria Jokl, who is in Jerusalem visiting from Berlin. She is mulling emigrating to Israel altogether, risking in her fifties changing her life once again, changing both home and work. She wants to learn a new language, to adapt herself to this new environment that appealed to her straightaway on her first trip to Israel in 1957. She paid a visit to Buber on her first trip to Jerusalem and they have remained in close contact since. He has made the world of Hasidism familiar to her, as he has for so many, with his stories and histories of Eastern European Jewry in the crown lands of Austria-Hungary, from which Jokl herself originates. Buber is the foster father of her move from Berlin to Jerusalem.

The Greenspan family opened Café Atara on Ben Yehuda Street in 1938 as a local eatery. It rapidly became a meeting place for the Yekkes, where the *MB* and *Das Pariser Tageblatt*, the *Jüdische Rundschau* from Berlin and *Die Weltwoche* from Zürich were laid out alongside the English-language *Jerusalem*

Post and the *Jedioth Chadaschoth*, bringing their readers ever grimmer news from their homelands. In its externals the Atara (Hebrew for 'crown') looked in 1961 much as it had when the café was first established two decades earlier: here still are the green awning, the brown coffee bean logo, the simple tables and chairs and the 'café hafuch' or 'upside-down coffee', a little coffee in a lot of milk, probably a Viennese invention from when the Turks left behind some sacks of coffee beans after the siege of the city – or the 'yerushalmi', for which you simply tossed ground coffee into the pot and then poured hot water over it.

The Atara was 'a piece of home for the Yekkes', recalls Gad Granach:

> People went to the Café to see and be seen. Everyone knew everyone. The young people sat upstairs on the first floor of the old Atara. The older folk, who could no longer manage the stairs, sat below. And everyone had 'his' waitress. These weren't little temp girls, they were seasoned women, many of whom had worked there for years. I remember Stella and Zima, who not only knew exactly what each of their regular customers always ordered but acted as mother confessors as well. I suspect that some of the guests talked more with them than with their own wives.

Scholem has arrived at Café Atara. He opens the glass door, catches sight of Buber and his unknown female companion. Buber introduces her: Anna Maria Jokl from Berlin. She casts a watchful but friendly eye over this tall man and extends her hand to him: 'Shalom.' Scholem sits himself down and orders coffee and chocolate cake, in this café where he has hardly ever been seen.

Buber begins without preamble. 'Permit me to say, straight-away and frankly, Herr Scholem, that your word "tombstone" for my Bible translation weighs heavily on my heart. I may guess what you wished to convey on that winter evening in my own home, but this hard, severe, stone-heavy word is ill-suited to my labour of years, of decades; it is unseemly to speak of it in this way.' He draws breath, but without permitting Scholem a chance to speak. 'The project of rendering the Bible from ancient Hebrew into German goes back decades, to when I, together with Franz Rosenzweig, first began it in Frankfurt. That was the natal hour of a living work, not a tombstone, as it appears now to you.'

'You do me an injustice, Herr Buber. This word "tomb-stone" relates not to your intention, which I esteem highly, just as I esteem that of Rosenzweig, nor to your labour as such, but rather to their effect today, thirty-five years later.' Scholem softens his voice and raises his index finger. 'I knew the danger that I would be misunderstood that evening in February. I could not but fear – or hope? – as I said in your home, that I would provoke you to contradict me. And yet this question forced itself upon my feelings: for whom is this translation now intended? In what medium will it have an effect? Historically considered, it is no longer a guest-gift from the Jews to the Germans, but instead – and it is not easy for me to say this – the tombstone of a relationship extinguished in unspeakable horror.' He allows his hand with its raised finger to fall. 'The Jews for whom you have made your translation no longer exist. Their children, those who escaped this horror, will no longer read German. The German language itself has been profoundly transformed in the space of a generation – as anyone who has had contact with the new German in recent years knows – and not in the direction of that linguistic utopia to which your enterprise bears such impressive witness. The gap between the real-world language of 1925 and your translation has by now, thirty-five years later, grown not smaller but larger.' In point of fact, Scholem already fiercely criticised Buber's translation back in the 1920s.

Buber looks across apologetically at his female companion, but he cannot let this stand. Jokl gives him a nod. She is curious as to his response. Buber speaks. 'But you know, Herr Scholem, that my true concern is for dialogue, conversation, exchange, controversy, even over the abyss. A conversation's failure belongs to it as much as its success; mismeeting is a part of meeting. Dialogue is a driving, scrutinising principle, not merely an isolated event. That is why I travelled back to Germany so very soon after 1945, in spite of the many opposing voices, yours included, and spoke to Germans, talked with politicians like Theodor Heuss, received awards like the Peace Prize of the German Book Trade. Life is meeting.'

Scholem responds. 'That is why, dear Herr Buber, I called your translation a guest-gift of the Jews to the Germans at the moment of their separation, before 1933, a guest-gift which the hosts most certainly spurned.'

Both gentlemen, the older as the younger, are speaking a German – tinged for one with Vienna, the other with Berlin – that today you never hear, and back then in Germany would seldom have heard: refined, erudite, elevated, earnest and without irony, with a pathos of distance that keeps the two far apart, and yet in their form binds them together.

The dispute drags on. Jokl is following it, but in the end politeness compels her to bring it to a close. She talks about her life in Berlin, her work as a psychotherapist. In the meantime, the café has filled. Hannah Arendt has seated herself at another table. She has just arrived from New York and taken lodgings in Rehavia to report on the trial of Adolf Eichmann, which will begin on 11 April 1961 at the Jerusalem District Court. The trial will agitate and preoccupy Israeli society for a long time; it preoccupies it to this day. Eichmann, one of the key architects of the Shoah, was captured and taken into custody by Mossad, the Israeli secret service, in May 1960. The *New Yorker* has sent Arendt to Israel to report on the trial in five instalments. She will publish her report, under the title *Eichmann in Jerusalem*, in English in 1963 and soon after that in German. This book will lead to a rancorous controversy between its author and her Israeli and American colleagues, most especially between her and Scholem. Their relationship will end in silence – an eloquent silence after a final break in lucid letters between them. But on this Shabbat evening, this lies for them in the future, for us in the past.

Mascha Kaléko steps briskly into the café. She knows who Arendt is, knew her fleetingly in New York, but the two women are worlds apart in how they see the world, in their writing and origins. So Kaléko does not approach her. A café in Jerusalem, she once wrote to a friend in America, is a slight euphemism. She has never felt at home here since she moved to Rehavia in 1959 with her husband, the composer of Hasidic music Chemjo Vinaver. She had hoped the mild climate would relieve the symptoms of his asthma; in reality they are both tormented by it, especially by the Khamsin, a föhn-like wind that, true to its Arabic name, meaning 'fifty', swathes the city in scorching heat for around fifty days a year, in early summer and autumn especially. Kaléko will always be an outsider in Jerusalem, just as Berlin, her home city, will never again feel familiar to her after the war. And yet this 'Grunewald of the East' lies even further from New York, home to her beloved only son. Every day she waits for a letter from Steven. But he hardly ever writes, and transcontinental telephone calls cost a fortune. So Kaléko lives in Rehavia with a thousand thoughts of New York and memories of Bleibtreustraße and the square around Savignyplatz in Berlin. Around this time, she writes from Jerusalem to a female friend:

> I heard a song on the radio from the late twenties in Berlin and it was like a thunderbolt, smashing open my slumbering feelings. In an instant my heart was again as it was then, so young, so roaring, so loving – that was *me* once, I thought, almost amazed.

Kaléko is working hard to get her once-so-popular books reissued and to place a new title with the publisher Rowohlt. In Berlin, Hamburg or Munich she finds her readers; in Israel no one knows her. In the café on Ben Yehuda Street she walks up to Scholem, Buber and Jokl's table. Scholem's Berlin inflections pierce her heart, and she is close to Buber; the two have corresponded. Jokl may be familiar with Kaléko's poems. They exchange a few words.

As the evening wears on, those of the scattered guests who know each other resolve to amalgamate. The waitresses put tables and chairs together. Arendt sits between Buber and Scholem – whom she calls only Gerhard; he calls her Hannah. Both stick with the formal 'you'. Jokl and Kaléko sit opposite. Werner Kraft joins the circle and takes a seat next to the two women, even though he finds the poetry of both too light on its feet, too of today, too close to life. Kraft's interest lies with the work of Stefan George, Rudolf Borchardt and the classics from Weimar. And yet here they are, sitting side by side.

Other evening guests form clusters at nearby tables. Lea Goldberg has entered the café. She teaches comparative literature at the Hebrew University. It is a prominent subject in Jerusalem, since most of the students have a different mother tongue alongside their Hebrew: Polish, Russian, German. Goldberg's own first language is Russian, but she is at home in the languages of the world, translates from Russian and Italian, writes and illustrates children's books and produces poems and essays as well. She sits down with Yehuda Amichai, who originates from Würzburg and at this point is barely thirty-seven years old but will later become the poetic voice of his country. Gad Granach, son of the actor Alexander Granach and a temperamental chronicler of his generation, who immigrated to Palestine in the 1930s, is drinking a coffee. And a little further away at another table a shy student sits alone. His kibbutz has sent him back to his hometown to study, a rare privilege granted to only the most gifted kibbutzniks. He was born Amos Klausner. As Amos Oz, forty years from now, he will produce one of the greatest books about Jerusalem, *A Tale of Love and Darkness*.

Happenstance has brought these people together in this café. They have come to this country by distinct and various routes over great distances, some for a short time, others forever; some out of conviction, inspired by Zionism, others under compulsion.

The dessert plates have been cleared. People drink coffee or tea; cosmopolitan Arendt has ordered a whisky, which they don't have, and is brought instead an Israeli brandy, brand-name 'Carmel'. There are sandwiches on the table, filled with the two kinds of cheese then available in Israel, the yellow and the white. There is salad. There is hummus and tahini, the chickpea puree and sesame paste derived from Arab cuisine.

The six swap views. They talk of where they came from, how they came to Rehavia, their lives in it; of Germany, the tensions between Israel and the Arabs, national politics and that eternal theme: the divided city. Scholem listens at first, then speaks a great deal: 'If something's gonna be said 'ere, I'm sayin' it', as they say in Berlin. Kraft, with his earnest literary sensibility, talks about a reading – it must have been in the early 1940s – where the now-forgotten poem 'All Souls' Day' by Hermann von Gilm was read aloud:

I remember how Else Lasker-Schüler concluded her speech before a reading in Jerusalem by quoting the first verse –

"Place the fragrant mignonettes on the table here,
Put the last red asters on display,
And let us talk again of love, dear,
As once we did in May."

– and all of shattered Germany awoke in those lines.

How vividly in this we see the significance of the German language for Rehavia, a past in quotation marks, split by a chasm from the reality of German as it was then spoken and written.

Else Lasker-Schüler was one of the founders, the inventors of this place as literature. Her imaginary Jerusalem was the actual Rehavia and the 'Kraal' – the literary club she organised. She was as well acquainted with Adon (that is, the Hebrew 'Mr') Scholem as with Adon Buber.

'A great poet. You know her haunts were just around the corner?' Kaléko recalls. 'The evening landscapes really are like the ones L[asker]-S[chüler] invented. She imagined them before she knew them. In her "Evening Colours of Jerusalem", I believe, she described something long before she was acquainted with it (except from the Bible and from paintings). Besides, what is a poet, if not someone who imagines? Imagines, not imitates.'

All these figures – almost – could have encountered each other in this café on this particular Shabbat evening. But, in fact, they did not. Sometime in the spring of 1961 Scholem travelled to London for several months and missed Arendt in Jerusalem; he learned about the opening and progress of the Eichmann trial from afar. Jokl was there a few years earlier and again later, before she moved entirely to Jerusalem in 1965.

By chance they were absent and yet they belong, of necessity, to any picture of Rehavia at the beginning of the 1960s.

It's late. The waitresses are beginning to put chairs on tables; the café is emptying; our group is leaving the Atara.

Someone escorts Buber to his taxi – the walk to his house would be too far for him. The remaining five head out on foot through the sleeping quiet of Rehavia. Together at first, then split. Scholem makes a right turn onto Abarbanel Street. Arendt says her goodbyes on King George Street and walks into her hotel. Kaléko lives at number thirty-three. 'Buber and his sort live around the corner,' she remarks. Kraft, who accompanies Scholem for some of his journey, turns into Alfasi Street, where he lives. Jokl has found lodgings near to Balfour Street, where later she will live for many years, opposite the Schocken Library and right next to the residence of the Israeli Prime Minister.

Rehavia as a Way of Life and Thought

Walk along the shady streets of Rehavia today and you will discover a prosperous district in the west of Jerusalem, with well-kept green spaces; quiet side streets; two traffic-filled main roads; little cafés on the two boulevards, Ramban and Ben Maimon; a mini-supermarket and a florist; a guest house called 'A Little House in Rehavia'; kiosks and a lotto booth; and a well-arranged bookshop on the corner. At the playground you will see devout parents with their children and hear that they are speaking French. Rehavia, once a secular neighbourhood, today draws many religious families. The Israeli Prime Minister's residence is the former Villa Aghion, built in 1938 by Richard Kauffmann.

Here and there, an isolated plaque indicates the history of a building – such as that on the corner of Ramban and Arlozorov Streets where the Bonem family commissioned a home from Leopold Krakauer, built between 1935 and 1936. The architect combined the functional modernism of the Bauhaus with an indigenous architecture that he discovered in the countryside, a combination of unadorned stone and oriental mosaic, of Arabian country houses and crisp cubes with small, plain windows, doors and balconies, bringing openness and dynamism to the rustic style. A patio, though open to the sky, has the feeling of an enclosed space. For forty years this architectural gem has been home to a bank. The terraces, balconies and garden no longer survive, but we still have the ground plan. Cash machines stand in the vestibule now, but in the banking hall someone has placed some of the original furniture.

At first glance, a visitor might imagine themselves in a Bauhaus building of the early 1930s in Weimar or Berlin. The mosaic floor has been restored; panels tell the story of the house. Bank Leumi has been mindful of its history and diligent in its conservation – an exception in Rehavia, where only rare traces recall the history and significance of the neighbourhood.

Not far from the bank branch in the Bonems' villa, the house at 28 Abarbanel Street is decaying. Here Gershom Scholem lived with his wife, Fania, for over forty-five years, until his death in February 1982. Here he composed an oeuvre that to this day astounds and puzzles the literary world. The house next to it is faring no better. These streets – Binyamin Mi-Tudela, Saadia Gaon, Abarbanel, Alfasi, Al-Harizi, Bartenura, Ramban – were named after scholars and poets of pre-1492 Spain, and serve as reminders of Rehavia's first homeowners: prosperous and educated oriental Jews.

Rehavia was intended as a garden city on the European pattern, generously laid out, with gardens to the rear of the houses and narrower gardens in front, a neighbourhood full of trees, hedges and flowers, with green spaces on the edges of the invitingly broad boulevards and parks on all sides. It was meant to be – and here there is no ignoring the Biblical resonance – a part of the new Jerusalem.

'The Rehavia residential district is situated on the main

street of the new Jerusalem. It is a part of the city proper and is situated near the train station and central shopping area,' reads a prospectus on the merits of this new area of the city, distributed by the Settlers' Society in 1930. It continues:

> The widest of Jerusalem's streets, King George Street, runs along its eastern border, connecting Rehavia with the train station and Jaffa Street, the main artery of the city. In the centre of Rehavia lies Ramban Street, the direct continuation of Mamilla Street, which links the central shopping area with the city's two grand hotels, the King David and the Palace, and with the Central Post Office and the Jaffa Gate. On its northern side Rehavia borders an array of West Jerusalem's Hebraic residential areas […] Rehavia is a garden city. Two thirds of every plot of land is reserved for vegetable and flower gardens, for cultivation and for the circulation of air. [The garden city] attracts a wide range of people who are linked to the city by their work and yet want to live in a neighbourhood of gardens and abundant fresh air.

In 1926, Lübeck, the Free Hanseatic City of pointed gables, celebrated its seven hundredth anniversary. When Thomas Mann, a native of the city, delivered his famous address 'Lübeck as a Way of Life and Thought' to an audience of dignitaries in the town hall as part of the celebrations, thousands of kilometres away there was a neighbourhood taking shape to which Mann's image of a way of life imbued with culture, intellectual connections, reading, writing, research, music and fine art could very happily be applied. This was not Lübeck's urban culture, evolved over centuries, which its famous son surveyed with both pride and a gentle irony, but a way of life that borrowed models from the Weimar Republic and the time of the Kaiser, and gave them new form and new substance.

Arrival of the Architects

On 28 March 1921 a young architect wrote from Berlin to 'Herr Richard Kauffmann, Zionist Commission, Jerusalem': 'Dear Herr Kauffmann! I learn from my sister Rosa Cohn that you are interested in making connections with Zionist architects available to work in Palestine. That I for my part am very interested in making your acquaintance, is clear enough; it is the purpose of my letter.'

So began the application letter of Lotte Cohn, in which she first contacted the man who was later to be her boss in Jerusalem, the man who had been at that point the senior city and settlement planner for the Palestine Land Development Company for only a few months. As a young architecture graduate, Kauffmann, after studying with the famous Theodor Fischer in Munich, had assisted with the design of the garden city of Margaretenhöhe in Essen. In Essen he met Lotte's brother Emil Cohn, then serving as a rabbi there. After the First World War, Kauffmann worked for a year and a half in Norwegian Kristiania, today's Oslo, from where in August 1920 he heard the summons to Palestine.

Cohn, a doctor's daughter from a bourgeois family, both Jewish and Zionist, wrote a disarmingly frank and open application letter:

I know that for the moment there is little prospect of me finding employment there. But should at any time an opportunity present itself, I would be quite happy to begin in some sort of technical position and learn how things work there from the ground up. This letter is, I imagine, detailed enough; I ask you to believe me that it is entirely sincere, far more candidly + objectively written than is usual with such statements. I emphasise this because I know from experience that application letters are, as a rule, read with a sceptical eye. It is my candid wish to establish a real understanding with you. For should this letter really at some point become the foundation of a professional relationship between you + me, any deception would be perilous for both parties. I am fully aware of this responsibility.

A few months later, at the end of July 1921, Cohn received a telegram from Jerusalem: 'OFFER ASSISTANT POSITION TEMPORARY TWENTY POUNDS MONTHLY, TRAVEL GRANT 25 POUNDS APPLY VISA IMMEDIATELY, PLEASE WIRE RESPONSE PLDC KAUFFMANN ZIONSCOM.'

And on the same day Kauffmann wrote his future assistant a letter as well:

My dear Fräulein Cohn! If I think of the yearning with which I came to this land, and even more so to the work in it – I was longing for it every moment – and of my joy when, last August in Norway, I learned of my appointment here, then I can imagine something of how you may now be feeling.

Kauffmann expressed his joy and his hope that he had made the right choice with Cohn. The city planning projects are queuing up, he wrote, 'of a scale and beauty and significance for the development of the country that compels a person to dedicate himself cheerfully, unconditionally and unreservedly to the task.' And in a postscript the sender added perhaps the most important point:

> Please bring with you, if you are at all able, some examples of exemplary *modern German building codes*. For cities and *garden cities*. Those for Essen (Schmidt), Hamburg (Schumacher), perhaps Cologne (Rehorst and Schumacher) would be *very good*. Then Hellerau and Taut's garden city (Falkendorf?). Also please some good contemporary literature, at our cost. Go see Taut. Bruno Taut is a great friend of Zionism!

On Thursday, 18 August 1921 the two sisters, Helene and Lotte Cohn, set out for Palestine from Berlin's Anhalter Station. On 4 September they travelled the last stretch of their long journey on the 'Orient Express', a small rickety bus riding the dusty unsurfaced road from Tel Aviv to Jerusalem. The hot desert wind tormented both sisters, Lotte especially. 'But as we arrived, the weather turned and I was able to take in a deep breath of Jerusalem's fresh mountain air.'

The Twenties in Eretz Israel is a 'Picture Book Without Pictures' by Lotte Cohn, 'written for the friends who lived through it with me', a retrospective which conjures a kaleidoscope of images and individual scenes concretely and vividly. Cohn was a resolute and powerful chronicler of her time, her surroundings and her friends, while being thoroughly unassuming and down-to-earth in regard to herself. It is the life story of a vocation, to become the 'Woman Master Architect of the Land of Israel', as her biographer Ines Sonder calls her.

If someone were to ask me what was special, what was characteristic of this small world of Jews on the soil of Eretz Israel, I would answer: "It was a world exclusively of the young. There was no one old among us. A reality infused with youthful life. Anyone who did not experience it with us can hardly imagine the charm of that narrow world." The reminiscences of those early immigrants almost always mention their youth. Many had succeeded in emigrating against the opposition of their parents. They carried on alone, relying on themselves: "We heard no 'in my day'… yet we felt all the more strongly our personal responsibility."

Cohn's memoir covers her first years in Jerusalem, before she relocated her architecture practice to Tel Aviv. She describes her first walk in Jerusalem, up Mount Scopus, on which, four years later, the Hebrew University would be established:

There she lies, my city Jerusalem, in all her magic, with her domes and churches, her mosques and minarets, history made stone, and what a history! The scenery slides in behind this unique image: the slope of the Mount of Olives with its ancient Jewish cemetery… if those old stones still lie there today? And we climb on up Scopus, a tree-covered landscape with a couple of old buildings. They are not breathtakingly beautiful, these houses, far from it, if anything they are pretty shabby; but how wonderfully they have grown out of this harsh soil, are themselves harsh and austere, with their cubic silhouettes. We have made it to the summit and now the view opens out to the East: Never forget this, hold it fast, this image. An undreamt-of panorama spreads itself before you, wave upon wave of mountain chain lies before you, drawn with clean, austere lines, here and there the gnarled form of an olive tree, a peculiar thicket of thistles, a large-leafed fig tree. Here is a derelict well shaft, there a romantic ruined wall, no doubt the marker of a property boundary... More and more details vanish as your eye penetrates further, down, down, to the place where you can see in the distance a dully shimmering lake in the desert, the Dead Sea. The reflection of the setting sun makes the otherworldly mountains glow pink gold. And now the moon is rising and the sky becomes a glowing red bell.

In late summer 1921, when Cohn went on her first hike up Mount Scopus, Rehavia was still countryside, a building plot; it was an idea. The network of streets had just been extended, a mains water supply and street lighting had been installed, and a city plan and building regulations were being developed – which was why Cohn had brought all those plans in her bulky luggage.

The new neighbourhoods of the rapidly growing city spread out predominantly to the west and northwest of the city walls, along the line of Jaffa Street, the old trade route to the sea, to Jaffa and Tel Aviv. Neither the Central Post Office nor the legendary King David Hotel had yet been built. Cohn had arrived in a barely developed country, which had awoken from the long slumber of Ottoman rule and now desperately needed architects, technicians, engineers and construction workers for its infrastructure. At first she worked with Kauff-mann on plans and projects for settlements and buildings outside of Jerusalem. But as chronicler, architect and resident, she belongs to the very heart of Rehavia. Three Cohn sisters had come to the country: Helene, Rosa and Lotte. The oldest of them, Helene, was born in 1882 in Steglitz, today a part of Berlin. Rosa was born in 1890. Lotte three years later. Three brothers, Max, Emil and Elias, joined them, but they struck out on different paths and did not come to Palestine. The sisters remained single and childless for their whole lives.

The parents of these six siblings, Cäcilie and Bernard Cohn, were among the rare representatives of the German-Jewish middle classes who shared their children's Zionist ideals; the children called their father a 'self-made Zionist'.

Rosa Cohn had already made the journey to Jerusalem at the end of 1920 to work as a secretary at the Jewish National Fund. Helene Cohn came in the summer of 1921 to work as a lab technician at the Rothschild Hadassah Hospital, until the early 1930s, when she opened the legendary Pension Helene Cohn at 28 Abarbanel Street. 'Modern Conveniences. Excellent Cuisine. Dietic Food to order' read her advertisement in English. She served cakes, sandwiches and hot and cold meals and provided catering for receptions in the city. And at the bottom it read, in the language of Rehavia, 'Feiner Mittags-tisch' ('Quality Lunch Table').

One leaflet for German clientele from a few years later praises the 'quiet, cool location, garden and roof terrace, beautiful, modern rooms with running water' and 'reasonable prices'.

Over many years, thousands of visitors from Europe and elsewhere overseas found shelter in Rehavia at the Pension Helene Cohn.

Käsebier takes Jerusalem

'Rehavia is its own world,' wrote Gabriele Tergit in one of her articles from the 1930s:

> At its entrance, the citadel of the Zionist authorities, a magnificent stone building with Assyrian touches. In front, cypresses, each one dedicated to a founder of Zionism. Rehavia, city of prosperous villas, laid out in a European style according to an English building code. Front gardens, modern houses, smooth and straight, two to three storeys high, made of local stone, pale grey ashlars, with flat terraced roofs and broad windows, loggias with slit openings, garages to the side, all with running water, tiled bathrooms, central heating for the rainstorm-heavy winter, fly nets, stone floors for the scorching summer, all still with no trees or lawns.

Tergit followed her husband, the architect Heinz Reifenberg, to Jerusalem in November 1933 and wrote up her impressions of the foreign city just as if she were carrying on with her reporting on Berlin or other cities.

Her eyes scanned the façades to expose each building's insides. Every detail contributed to a larger observation:

The middle-class interior, bookcase, couch, standard lamp and buffet. Ladies who get themselves ready and ladies who play bridge. Bourgeois betrothal, marriage and dowry. Rehavia is a city of officials and academics. That's just what it is. The normalisation of the Jewish people has created Jewish bureaucracy. Narrow, career-obsessed, salary-obsessed, patriotic, chauvinist, arrogant.

Nothing escaped Tergit, neither the hierarchy of the Zionist organisation for which someone worked nor the salary they earned for doing so, nor how long they had been in the country, nor the disparity between secular and religious Judaism:

Between Rehavia and the Wailing Wall no bridge exists. Lamentation for the lost Temple has been abandoned. Rehavia is seen as a conclusion. It is safety. It is homeland and return. The Jew with his eyes on millennia seems obsolete and eccentric in this cheerful city. It's a daring people that names a movie house "Cinema Zion".

The first – and for a long time only – cinema in Jerusalem, the Zion was centrally located on Jaffa Street and showed European and American films. Gershom Scholem reported to his mother in August 1930 that the roof of the cinema could be 'folded back on beautiful summer days – and when are they not here?'

Close to Cinema Zion stands – still to this day, though the cinema has long since been demolished – one of the city's pivotal places: the Central Post Office, for decades the most important transfer hub for messages arriving from outside Jerusalem, be they telegrams, letters or phone calls. Our reporter Tergit – our artist of reportage, rather – shows us the international multitudes by way of its queue:

> ... the kavasses, the servants of the consulates, in long Turkish trousers, some in raw silk, with buttoned jackets and broad red sashes across the body; the Italian kavass in blue, silver-embroidered cloth with red and silver brocade circling a red fez; an English reverend; old Jews in long velvet coats and fur hats; old Jews in striped robes with long black skirts; Scotsmen in short plaid skirts, red and white socks, white gaiters, small caps; policemen with black fur caps and short khaki trousers; a Jewish woman in a flowery summer dress and large hat; a brown Franciscan with bare feet, cowled robe, cord around the waist and pith helmet; an Arab in lounge suit and fez; an Arab in a long robe and white headscarf; a Catholic wearing a pith helmet; a Frenchman with a broad black sash around his priest's cassock. A German evangelical deaconess; an Arab sheikh in white robes, white coat, white headscarf with a golden band around it; an Arab woman from the country-side in a long linen dress embroidered in red.

As colourfully and variously, officially and ceremonially as this plethora of costumes arises before our eyes, so too do the requests and addresses, the 'letters sent to high and solemn institutions', to the Vatican library, to the Chief Rabbi in New York, to the Franciscan friary in Assisi, to 10 Downing Street, to the governments of every European nation. And in the

Central Post Office in the winter of 1943, Else Lasker-Schüler dispatches a telegram, of which we do not know whether it reached its addressee: 'MARSHAL STALIN KREMLIN STALINGRAD. YOU ARE THE BRAVEST AND LOVELIEST PERSON IN THE WORLD. THE POETESS ELSE LASKER-SCHÜLER.'

Of Love and Darkness

The pioneer spirit of the mostly young immigrants of the 1920s gave way within a decade to distress, deprivation and the homesickness and painful separations of Jews who had emigrated to Palestine after the Nazis had come to power. They had often only the barest necessities and were fearful for family members they had had to leave behind in Germany, because only one of them had received the coveted certificate.

Some children succeeded in bringing their aged parents to Palestine. The question arose of whether a person came because of Germany or Zionism, out of necessity or conviction, fleeing or migrating. The dream city was invaded by nightmares, painful memories of traumatic experiences in the homeland, anxiety and hardship. In September 1941 the author Asher Beilin wrote about 'Our Yekkes':

Every day on the quiet streets of Jerusalem I meet assorted specimens of this tribe. The scholars and artists, who live among us on a deserted island, cut off, no one asks after them or pays attention to them. The lonely old women and men, stooped, who are filled with fear for their children caught in the claws of the demonic enemy and for whom there is no consolation. People of every age who are struggling to survive. I have seen how they sell off their households piece by piece – the Shabbat candles, the silverware or a clock, things they had salvaged from their hostile country. I have seen how they have sold off their individual souls, whom they loved truly and intimately, their friends, who are exactly as mute as they are – their dogs – because they are unable to pay for a dog licence. I have been witness to suicides, born of loneliness, fear of hunger and unbearable sorrow; fine, delicate souls, who chose death over a sorrow-filled life.

This generation in Jerusalem was a generation often lost, lost between times, the time of its old home and its new one, between memories and the demands of the present. Its chronicler was Amos Oz. 'I was born and bred in a tiny, low-ceilinged ground-floor flat,' begins his *A Tale of Love and Darkness*, a book of the century, the book of his life, which opens in the year 1939, when Oz was born in Kerem Avraham, a district next door to Rehavia. For little Amos, Rehavia was where the rest of the world began:

> With the passage of the years I became aware that Jerusalem, under British rule in the nineteen-twenties, thirties and forties, must be a fascinatingly cultured city. It had big businessmen, musicians, scholars and writers: Martin Buber, Gershom Scholem, S.Y. Agnon, and a host of other eminent academics and artists. Sometimes as we walked down Ben Yehuda Street or Ben Maimon [Boulevard] my father would whisper to me: "Look, there is a scholar with

a world-wide reputation." I did not know what he meant. I thought that having a world-wide reputation was somehow connected with having weak legs, because the person in question was often an elderly man who felt his way with a stick and stumbled as he walked along, and wore a heavy woollen suit even in summer.

The Jerusalem my parents looked up to lay far from the area where we lived: it was in leafy Rehavia with its gardens and its strains of piano music, it was in three or four cafés with gilded chandeliers in the Jaffa Road or Ben Yehuda Street, in the halls of the YMCA or the King David Hotel, where culture-seeking Jews and Arabs mixed with culti-vated Englishmen with perfect manners, where dreamy long-necked ladies floated in evening dresses, on the arms of gentlemen in dark suits, where broad-minded Britons dined with cultured Jews or educated Arabs, where there were recitals, balls, literary evenings, *thés dansants*, and exquisite, artistic conversations. Or perhaps such a Jeru-salem, with its chandeliers and *thés dansants*, only existed in the dreams of the librarians, schoolteachers, clerks and bookbinders who lived in Kerem Avraham. At any rate, it didn't exist where we were. Kerem Avraham, the area where we lived, belonged to Chekhov.

Chekhov knew about the longing for another place, which in Kerem Avraham had only one direction: towards Rehavia. Amos's father, Yehuda Arieh Klausner, nephew of the famous scholar Joseph Klausner, had left Vilnius for Palestine with his parents Alexander and Shlomit in 1933 and enrolled in the master's programme in literature at the Hebrew University almost as soon as he arrived. Three years later he met his future wife, Fania, there. An emigrant from Prague, she was studying history and philosophy in Jerusalem. Amos's father craved an academic position his entire life, while working as a librarian. In 1970, the last year of his life, he was still negotiating a lectureship in literature in Beer-Sheva, where later the Ben-Gurion University would be established, the university which sixteen years later appointed his son Amos professor and a few years after that installed him in a chairmanship named after S.Y. Agnon.

Amos's mother suffered from severe depression for years and took her own life on 6 January 1952. Two years later the fifteen-year-old Amos joined the Kibbutz Hulda and took the name Oz, Hebrew for strength.

Descended from Eastern European Jews on both his father's and mother's sides, Oz was a polyglot, learned and western-oriented. As an adolescent 'sabra' (that is, a Jew born in the land of Israel), Oz observed the German-Jewish world of Rehavia at a distance. It was a dream world a quarter of an hour's walk from Kerem Avraham and it seems as if it was precisely that distance that made his great novel of Jerusalem possible.

Gad Granach, an older man who came to Jerusalem in 1936 at the age of twenty-one, remembers the new city:

Jerusalem during the Mandate period was pure madness. It was, in a manner of speaking, the chief city of its era. Jerusalem was a genuinely cosmopolitan city. Ancient peoples had been marching through it for millennia: Romans,

Greeks, Persians, Babylonians, Arabs, Turks, Crusaders. The life was wild. There were parties, dances, chamber concerts and lectures. Today doesn't compare. The *Yekkes* had brought so much with them and they were trying to pick up in Palestine where they had left off in Germany. Tucholsky or Polgar spoke once of the tragedy of a bottle of medicine at a deathbed. That fits the place exactly.

Beginnings

From the beginning, Rehavia was an area of colourful social mixing. The upper-class Sephardi (that is, the Oriental Jewish families who had long resided in Jerusalem), lived alongside recently immigrated employees of Zionist organisations, who in turn worked for the Yishuv, the Jewish settlers. The most striking feature of the new district was the men walking through the city dressed in suits with collar and tie, the women in skirt suits, immigrants of German origin, people very much in the central European mould set against an oriental backdrop.

In November 1936, Nathan Alterman, the national poet of the emerging Jewish nation, published a poem in the *Haaretz* newspaper in Hebrew (Alterman forbade translation of his work into German).

From terrace to terrace, architects speak,
and doctor dwells opposite doctor…
Look and understand, my visiting friend:
Rehavia is burgeoning acre by acre –
Mimicry thrives and snobbism blossoms.
Boredom works miracles.

With good reason, urban historian Amnon Ramon entitled his book on Rehavia *Doctor Mul Doctor Gar*, which means – in slightly warped and poorly learned Hebrew – 'doctor dwells opposite doctor'.

With Lotte Cohn at his side, Richard Kauffmann planned several other 'garden settlements' in Jerusalem: Talpiot, Beit Hakerem, Bayit Vagan and Kiryat Moshe. But none of these other areas has preserved its original character quite like Rehavia.

The capture of Jerusalem by British troops in December 1917 signified the city's entry into modernity. The first British mandatory government under military direction (1917–1920) evolved plans for opening up and developing Jerusalem as it did for the whole country. In 1920 the civilian government allowed building to begin. The Ottoman land registers were updated and land ownership legally recorded. In February 1921 the first 'Town Planning Ordinance in Eretz Israel' was published.

The Balfour Declaration had spurred on the idea of a 'New Jerusalem'. In November 1917 the British Foreign Secretary Lord Arthur Balfour had assured Lord Rothschild, the representative of British Jews, that His Majesty's Government viewed 'with favour the establishment in Palestine of a national home for the Jewish people' and would do its best to bring this goal to fruition. A month later British troops under General Allenby took Jerusalem.

The idea of creating a Jewish nation state is much older, but British foreign and colonial policy gave it a decisive push towards realisation. And there was a second factor: after the October Revolution at the end of 1917 the stream of donations from Russian pilgrims dried up, contributing to the Greek

Orthodox Church going bankrupt. The Church had the largest holdings of land outside Jerusalem's city walls: 538,000 square metres, or around 490 dunams, spread across various parts of the city. This land was sold at auction to the highest bidders: the Jewish National Fund and the Jewish Colonisation Association. The so-called 'grand purchase' comprised parts of Talpiot and the 'Arab triangle' – today Ben Yehuda and King George Streets as well as the 'Janziria a-Fauqa' ('on top'), where Rehavia was later built. In spite of all protests by the Arab authorities and the Catholic Church, the Greek Orthodox Church transferred the territory to the Jewish National Fund and the Jewish Colonisation Association in a solemn ceremony held on 12 June 1922. The Greek Patriarch Damian blessed the new landowners. Arthur Ruppin, born in Rawicz (formerly in Prussia, now in Poland) and brought up in Magdeburg, gave a vote of thanks on their behalf. In the same year he wrote:

> I had hoped we would sell off the land at Rehavia and (what became) Ben Yehuda Street quickly so that we could cover our debt to the Patriarch. I myself bought a building plot in Rehavia in the hope I would inspire others to copy me. But the Jews of Jerusalem didn't really trust that stony and hilly site with no streets connecting it to Jerusalem proper. Though only a kilometre distant as the crow flies, the connections were so bad that the journey in from there took almost an hour.

The idea of the 'garden city' or 'garden suburb' fundamentally derives from Ebenezer Howard's book *Garden Cities of To-morrow* (1898), in which he promoted the idea of the garden city, as Theodor Fritsch had before him in Germany. Light, air and greenery were intended to offer respite, diversion and the comfort of a short commute to the inhabitants of the densely populated and polluted industrial cities of the late nineteenth century. For Howard, the garden city of Hellerau near Dresden set the standard.

The Jerusalem of the 1920s had nothing in common with England's large, sooty industrial cities. Richard Kauffmann, on his return from an extended tour of the garden cities of England, Holland and Germany at the end of 1922, nevertheless thought there could be 'no better form of settlement for our land, not only on practical, but also on social, health, moral and aesthetic grounds'. He had been impressed by the 'green lungs' and 'gardens for strolling' which vivified the garden city like a 'beating heart'. In contrast to the desolation of the great cities, the garden city embodied the ideal of a quiet place to both work and live, or, in short, 'the ideal form of life, bar none'.

Here Zionism's understanding of itself as a young and avant-garde movement, eager to attach itself to an advanced building style, came into play. In this way Kauffmann made the case for building Rehavia at a higher, more noble stage of development. In his first design for the neighbourhood, called Rehavia 1 or A, he drew out an area running from Keren Kayemet Le-Israel in the north to Ramban Street in the south and from King George Street in the east to Diskin Street in the west. The plan's backbone was a green pedestrian axis – today's Kuzari Garden – which divided the district running north–south. The axis began at the Rehavia Gymnasium in the north and ended at the playground on Ramban Street, today the Eliezer Yellin Garden. Long narrow streets (Al-Harizi and Arlozorov) branched off from the axis. The houses were to stand in large gardens, exuding a quiet, rural atmosphere. The shortcomings of this plan, which started out from the idea of a largely private, self-contained neighbourhood, only became apparent as the years passed. The narrow streets, originally laid out for strolling, became traffic-clogged arteries as Jerusalem grew.

The immigration of Jews fleeing Nazism in Germany enabled the neighbourhood to grow dramatically. In 1933 there were just 87 buildings and 705 residents; by 1936 that had roughly tripled to 246 buildings and 2,520 residents. Rehavia's directory for that year, a booklet of seventeen pages, records around 550 entries for families or unattached residents. The list of family names – Oppenheimer, Scholem, Herlitz, Koebner – and first names – Siegfried, Arthur, Theodor, Berthold, Fritz, Paula, Rosa and so on – testifies to their origin. There are a few Russian and Polish names. The list of professions – professor, teacher, doctor, civil servant – indicates the social structure. Only occasionally does one come across a hairdresser, perhaps, or a grocer or electrician. The manual workers in Rehavia – locksmiths, tailors, hairdressers, bakers, a florist, upholsterers – came as a rule from Poland, Lithuania and Russia. Having said that, women's manual labour is well represented in the directory. There is a seamstress – distinct from a female tailor – a pot painter, a female cook. There are only isolated Sephardi names, such as Abady, and no Arab names at all. At 21 Keren Kayemet Le-Israel lives one Adolf, surname Lustig, engineer.

With the so-called Fifth Aliyah, the wave of immigration from the early 1930s into the early 1940s, fifty to sixty thousand Jewish emigrants from Germany, Austria and Czechoslovakia arrived in the country. And of that old-new population, the smallest part, but an especially influential one, moved into Rehavia – or 'Yekkeland', as David Kroyanker calls it.

The Hebrew Gymnasium

The Rehavia Gymnasium, where Amos Oz studied, also known as the Hebrew Gymnasium, was the first port of call for those getting to know the neighbourhood. It was the second Jewish secondary school to open in Palestine after the Gymnasium of the same name in Tel Aviv. Originally established in the Bukharan Quarter, the school took possession of its current building on Keren Kayemet Le-Israel in 1929. Among its first teachers were Yitzhak Ben-Zvi – later the second President of the state of Israel, and a teacher and scholar after whom Jerusalem's urban history institute in Rehavia is named – and his wife Rachel Yanait. Its former pupils have included renowned scholars like Trude Dothan, writers like A.B. Yehoshua, politicians like Dan Meridor and the Israeli President Reuven Rivlin, and many others.

The word 'gymnasium' (in German an academically oriented secondary school) promises a classical, humanist education, but the Hebrew Gymnasium was closer to a training school for Zionists, covering not just Hebrew, Bible study, English and modern foreign languages but also mathematics, regional studies, psychology, sport and technical subjects.

Esther Herlitz, who was born in Berlin in 1921 and came to

Jerusalem with her parents in 1933, conveys the fierce opposition to the settling of Jewish families from Germany even
in Rehavia:

> I wanted to be a Sabra at any cost. I tried with all my
> strength to eradicate every Yekke trait that clung to me.
> I refused to speak German with my mother though she
> knew only a few words of Hebrew. The language was hard
> to master; she gave up. But the Sabras in my class [at the
> Hebrew Gymnasium] gave me and my three girlfriends,
> who barely spoke Hebrew and communicated with each
> other in German, no chance to integrate ourselves. They
> called us 'Nazis'. I didn't cry. I gave no sign of being
> offended. But I was atrociously angry. I went home and
> announced I was going on strike. I informed my parents
> that I would no longer be going to this school. I did
> not like the school and could not bear my schoolmates'
> behaviour. I couldn't understand Raschi's exegeses [in my
> religion class] either. I just wanted out. After a year, salva-
> tion appeared. The director of the Zionist School in Berlin
> came to Israel and opened a school in Talpiot. Thank God.
> The yekkish children rose up as one and switched school.

Thirteen-year-old Herlitz already had a traumatic school
year in Germany behind her, followed by this unpleasant
interlude in Rehavia, before she was able to go to the newly
established Hebrew University School in another part of Jerusalem. She emerged resilient, warm-hearted and dedicated
to the service of her country. She fought as an officer in the
British Army and in the Zionists' underground militia, the

Haganah. She later became Israel's ambassador to Denmark and retained a special connection to that country throughout her life. She was a member of the Knesset, Israel's parliament, for the Labor Party.

Not all yekkish children found the Hebrew Gymnasium so hostile. Ruth Lachmann, a schoolfellow of Herlitz's, had a quite different experience. Lachmann's father, Joseph Lachmann, was born on 10 November 1882 in Znin near Bromberg. Joseph's father, Nachman, had died when Joseph was five years old and his mother, Louise, was for a time alone with their six children before she married again and moved the family to Berlin. After graduating from the Humboldt Gymnasium, Joseph studied medicine and specialised in the then nascent field of ear, nose and throat medicine during a five-month-long internship at Berlin's Jewish Hospital. He became well established as a specialist in Berlin, but from early on he was trying to leave for Palestine and made several trips to the country. At first his desire to emigrate foundered on the lack of professional prospects there, and Joseph continued to live with his family on Motzstraße in Schöneberg, Berlin.

As the time of the Nazis approached, the American ambassador to Germany, who was a patient of his, offered for Joseph to emigrate to the USA, but he declined and emigrated with his wife, Valerie, and their two daughters to Palestine. There Joseph founded the ear, nose and throat department in the new Hadassah Hospital on Mount Scopus, and directed it until his retirement in 1952. In Rehavia the Lachmanns lived in the famous windmill.

Joseph and Valerie Lachmann's daughter Ruth had been born in Schöneberg, Berlin, on 19 November 1919, and she became an older sister to Evelin (Chava), born 1921. After school in Talpiot, where she was a schoolfellow of Esther Herlitz, Ruth attended the Hebrew Gymnasium. Her school report from 1937 has survived: for natural history and economics she was graded 'kim'at tov' – almost good; for history good; psychology, grammar, literature, English, French all almost good; algebra and geometry satisfactory; and then for the peculiar subject of 'medical literature' again good. There were subjects for Zionism and agricultural studies, and one for handicraft, but the latter is crossed out on the report, presumably omitted. Tanakh – in other words, Bible studies – good; Talmud satisfactory. For all the yekkish virtues – manners, leadership, attention and industry – she was very good. Ruth stayed on at the Hebrew Gymnasium.

Visitors

On 11 February 1925, Shmuel Hugo Bergmann, director of the National Library, was standing at Jerusalem train station with his wife, Else, waiting for exalted visitors: Franz Werfel and Alma Mahler were arriving for a stay of several weeks in Palestine. The couple had set off four weeks earlier on board the 'Vienna' from Trieste to Alexandria, then on to Cairo, Luxor, Thebes – Else Lasker-Schüler's 'Dream City' – and finally by train via El Qantara to Jerusalem. Werfel began a travel diary on 16 January 1925 to record his impressions. Right at the beginning he noted:

Jews on the boat, emigrating to Palestine. Two groups: old and young. An old man in Ghetto fur cap from the 16th century has been travelling with us since Vienna. Poignant. Seems an image of the fate of the Jewish past. Yet at the same time, he might almost be a farmer. The other: intellectual big city youth. But remarkably vital and clearly full of happy expectation, delight even. All travel third class. They loiter on the after deck. One of them (Alma calls him the Jewish Czokor) has a freshness that is quite unghettolike.

This last may have been the unknown singer on the ship: 'this Jewish vibrato with his decrescendoing fermata on the final note', 'a cross between bel canto and folk song'. He received great acclaim for his performance.

Werfel's description of his impressions – at first coherent, novelistic – soon acquired, especially after their arrival in Jerusalem, a jittery, nervous tone: 'From our first moment here I have been plunged into conflict. Describing my impressions no longer suffices. Indeed, looking at things occupies just a small part of our day. My hand is no longer free. My temper is no longer calm.'

His companion made a decisive contribution to his turmoil and unease by fulminating against both land and people. Werfel wrote: 'Alma is so dreadfully resistant to Jewishness here in itself and still more (needless to say) to Communist-Jewishness. I am perpetually being dragged into the false role of mediator, a polemicist for both sides. I am, in truth, being torn this way and that.'

These scenes from a future marriage (the couple wed in 1929) were scenes of a permanent mode of thought. In her autobiography *My Life* (the English version, which is somewhat different, is titled *And the Bridge is Love*), the notoriously antisemitic Alma Mahler-Werfel ranted about the improvised nature of the country, the dirty hotels, deficiencies on all sides. Of her visit to the Heftziba kibbutz, founded three years earlier, she wrote:

> The women were very poorly dressed. The place had barely begun and everything was still, as you might say, 'en negligé'. Tea was served in rusty eggcups. Then we walked out into the fresh air and they showed us the whole compound. Especially the nursery, which was the pride of the settlement. But flies and strong draughts blew over the helpless, motherless creatures.

Lotte Cohn witnessed the entry of these 'illustrious guests' into the Bergmanns' Jerusalem household:

> What prats! And in among the Jerusalem intelligentsia! Naturally they were straightaway taken hostage + worked over, because, yes, Franz Werfel really ought to write poems about us, which a thousand + one outsiders will be able to read and reread. [...] Incidentally, the Mahler widow is a well put together woman of the world of great, the greatest, elegance. She is robust to the point of vulgarity, in both her appearance and her social conduct, which is practised to the nth degree, and has a strong tinge of tomboyish Viennese cheek (what Berliners call *kess*).

The 'woman of the world' and Franz Werfel travelled to the Holy Land again in 1930, just six months after their wedding. Alma Mahler-Werfel recorded: 'We found that Palestine had grown tremendously, beautified itself and become far more interesting in the five short years we had not been there.' At Werfel's request the couple travelled on from Jerusalem to Damascus, Baalbek and Beirut. In Damascus they had themselves conducted around the largest of the carpet weaving factories, where the famished children, at work on the bobbins and threads, caught the eye of both visitors. Mahler-Werfel recalled:

> Franz Werfel asked the proprietor who these remarkable children were. "Oh, those poor creatures! I gather them up off the street and give them ten piastres a day to stop them starving to death. They're the children of Armenians slain by the Turks. If I didn't take them in here, they'd starve to death and no one would care."

Thus Franz Werfel's depiction of the murder of the Armenians in his classic novel *The Forty Days of Musa Dagh* had its origins in Damascus. Here Werfel first began to understand the fate of the Armenian people.

Another visitor in 1925 was Lotte Cohn's mother, Cäcilie, come from Berlin to see her three daughters in Jerusalem. She was, Lotte recalls, enthused from the first moment: 'To my amazement, the magic of this land, our home, our life among all the young people seized her immediately.'

Visitors gained first impressions of the country and its people that often helped them to emigrate later. Seven years after Cäcilie's first trip, when she visited her family in Jerusalem for the second time, she straightaway decided to stay on and never returned to Germany. Her daughters, with great prescience, had read the political signs correctly. Cäcilie died in Jerusalem in 1935.

Felix Salten journeyed to Palestine; Manfred Sturmann wrote a *Palestinian Diary*; Arthur Holitscher published his *Travels through Jewish Palestine* (1921). There were Zionist trips to the land of Israel as well as anti-Zionist, socialist, Christian and touristic trips. The 'isms' of the preceding century set sail for the Middle East, enthusiastic or sceptical but at any rate curious. Wolf Kaiser produced an entire book on these German-language travelogues.

'To all coming home to this land I wish the fulfilment of their ideals,' writes Oskar Kokoschka on 21 April 1929 in the visitors' book of Moshe Ya'akov Ben-Gavriêl's house in Jerusalem. The painter – he too had once been Alma's lover – was in Palestine for the first time, staying in the house of Ben-Gavriêl, who was born Eugen Höflich in Vienna and had given himself a new Hebrew name replete with resonances after he settled in Jerusalem in 1927. Ben-Gavriêl quickly became a renowned host. He knew both city and country well, having travelled to Jerusalem in March 1917 as an officer of a company in the Austro-Hungarian army defending the Ottoman troops fighting alongside the Germans against the British Army. The frontlines of the First World War ran across the Middle East as well.

Ben-Gavriêl wrote a book based on his experiences in 1917, full of humour and irony in one moment and then entirely serious the next. *Jerusalem is for Sale, or Gold in the Streets* – recently republished by Sebastian Schirrmeister – is a war novel as much as an anti-war novel, a burlesque on the comedy and lunacy of waging war. Ben-Gavriêl, Austrian and

Jew, was an early champion of Pan-Asianism, a now-forgotten ideology from the early twentieth century which emphasises the closeness and similitude of Jews and Arabs; Hermann Hesse was another among its many adherents. Ben-Gavriêl bathes Jerusalem especially in a luminous harmony of the two peoples. Under the bright Jerusalem moon, Arab and Jewish children sing their shared songs in their two languages. The author himself studied Arabic. Jews from old Europe, like himself, seemed to him an aberration of history, destined to return to their Asiatic origins in Palestine and to the harmony that awaited them there. After its eventual victory, the British Mandatory Power imposed a lengthy entry ban on his rebellious contemporaries and the then Eugen Höflich did not return to Jerusalem until 1927.

Ben-Gavriêl was a guide to the city but more especially to the world of his thoughts, a very busy journalist, spirited conversationalist and, as evidenced by the entries in his visitors' book, an unstinting host. In 1935 he entertained Mascha Kaléko, Else Lasker-Schüler and many others: those passing through, those tagging along and those newly arrived as much as those coming home.

He writes in one of his late poems:

The night over Jerusalem
is like a ball
that has no dome or ground
borderless skyless
suffused with depth
beyond the imaginable...

His novels *Mahaschavi in Peace and War* (1952) and *The Scandalous Life of Osman the Great* (1955), to name only two, earned Ben-Gavriêl acclaim as an 'inexhaustible storyteller' and 'Israel's Mark Twain'. His historically significant *The House on Karpfengasse*, set in German-occupied Prague in March 1939, became his best-selling book.

When Kokoschka returned to the land of Israel, more than forty years later, Ben-Gavriêl was no longer alive. He had died in September 1965, two days after his seventy-fourth birthday. In March 1973 the by then world-famous Kokoschka drew his 'Jerusalem Faces', faces moulded by the past as well as the present of that city and that land, and projecting into its future: Golda Meir, Foreign Minister and Prime Minister of Israel; Benedict I, Greek Orthodox Patriarch of Jerusalem; Sheikh Mustafa Khalil el-Ansari, chief warden of the Mosque of Omar; Teddy Kollek, legendary mayor of the city; and the Minister of Defence, Moshe Dayan.

Under the title 'A Nazi Travels to Palestine', Joseph Goebbel's newspaper *Der Angriff* ('The Attack') published a series of twelve articles by Leopold von Mildenstein on his six-month-long trip to Palestine. 'What is the future for this land? What are the prospects for Zionism in the turbulent East? Is this where the solution to the Jewish question is to be found?' So the series begins, its tone sanctimoniously neutral and sober. Subscribers to the newspaper received a medal inscribed with the words 'A Nazi Travels to Palestine', a swastika and a Star of David. It is one of the most grotesque stories in the history of National Socialism, a history rich in grotesquery. Von Mildenstein detects 'something new in the nature' of the Zionist pioneers: 'It lifts their shoulders, enables them to raise up that lowered ghetto glance.' He writes of a 'degenerate people being restored to health by putting down new roots in old soil' and concludes, 'The new Jews are becoming a new people.' A Nazi travels to Palestine in the service of domestic propaganda. The aim was to compel German Jews to emigrate to Palestine by any means – including persuasion.

Leopold Itz, Edler von Mildenstein was born in Prague in 1902, scion of old Bohemian aristocratic stock. He worked as a journalist on the *Berliner Börsen-Courier* ('Berlin Stock Exchange Courier'), became a member of the Nazi Party in 1929 and joined the SS in 1932. He seems to have made several trips to the Middle East. His journey to Palestine allowed him to present himself as an expert. Reinhard Heydrich gave him the rank SS-Untersturmführer ('Junior Storm Leader') in the 'Jewish Affairs' department of the SD (Security Service) Main Office. Von Mildenstein brought Adolf Eichmann into the department; Eichmann went on to set up the 'Jews Section' in the Reich Security Main Office. At the end of 1936, following conflict with Heydrich, von Mildenstein quit his position and resumed his travels.

From 1938 he directed the Middle East department of the Reich Propaganda Ministry, responsible for pro-Arab propaganda, predominantly directed against the British Mandatory Power in Palestine. In the same year, his book *Around the Burning Land of the Jordan* appeared in Berlin, with accounts of his travels in Libya, Egypt, Greece, Iraq, Syria and Palestine:

The nearer we get to Palestine, the more agitated the passengers become. Alongside a whole array of Jewish tourists, wishing, as they put it, to behold Palestine once, we took on board in Athens an assortment of Eastern-Jewish migrants. For them in Jaffa a great decision awaits.

A lifetime later, in 2006, an Israeli filmmaker called Arnon Goldfinger was clearing out the flat of his grandmother Gerda, who had died aged ninety-eight. In amongst all the fur coats, handbags, cloths and towels, porcelain, books and editions of the classics which she had brought with her from Berlin, her grandson discovered a photo album showing his grandfather and grandmother in Palestine in 1933 in the company of von Mildenstein and his wife.

Kurt and Gerda Tuchler had travelled to Palestine with the von Mildensteins on behalf of the Zionist Federation of Germany. For promotional purposes, the car firm Opel had supplied them with a vehicle, which the two couples drove around Palestine, from Haifa to Tel Aviv: 'Only Jews live here. Only Jews work here. Only Jews do business, swim and dance here,' writes von Mildenstein of that Hebrew city. They drive to Jerusalem and visit a kibbutz. Von Mildenstein's articles veer between admiration and antisemitic Nazi clichés of simplicity, frugality and the primacy of the collective, which he thought he had found in Palestine.

The Tuchlers told their daughter Hannah about this journey only in passing, and only said that there was a German with them, not that he was a Nazi. Of the friendship they had established with the von Mildenstein couple they said nothing at all. The von Mildensteins took the Tuchlers to the train station when they emigrated to Palestine in 1936. Hannah only learned about her grandmother's death in a

German concentration camp from her son Arnon's research: 'They simply told us nothing. And we didn't ask.'

But that is not all: Arnon Goldfinger discovered, on the phone with Edda von Mildenstein, daughter of the friends of his grandparents, living in Wuppertal, that the Tuchlers had renewed their ties with the couple in Germany after the war. 'Of course I know them. They were good friends of my parents,' Edda reveals. 'They visited us here.' Leopold von Mildenstein pursued a career which could hardly have been typical for a Nazi in what was then West Germany: he became a member of the Free Democratic Party and a representative for Coca-Cola. At Adolf Eichmann's trial in Jerusalem in 1961, the defendant mentioned how smoothly he had collaborated with his superior, Leopold von Mildenstein.

Goldfinger resolved to travel to Germany to follow the traces of a friendship he had known nothing about. The death of his grandmother had brought the past back to life. So the 2011 Israeli film *The Flat* came into being. It caused a furore in Israel especially but also in Germany, forcing people to pay attention to history once more. It broke a great silence through its images even more than its words. The images made it possible to hear the story. The daughter Hannah says in flawless German – though she herself speaks only English – a saying her father Kurt Tuchler had passed on to her: 'Ein Todesfall ist kein Trauerfall.' A death is not a tragedy.

A Zionist Official

Amnon Ramon ascribes a number of attributes to this 'Prussian island in an Oriental sea': honesty, thoroughness, systematic rationalism, realism, even a certain lack of imagination, a dry sense of humour, no sharp elbows, courteous manners and a reverence for German culture, its literature and music, Bach and Mozart, Bechstein pianos and the violin. One might add that humour and irony are largely absent or at best delivered in fine doses. All attributes which still today are associated with the Yekkes, of whom there remain very few originals.

If you are seeking the ideal type of a Rehavite, one such would be the father of Esther Herlitz (who herself died in Jerusalem in March 2016). In the phone book, Dr Georg Herlitz listed his profession as 'archivist'. He had built up the Zionist archive in Berlin over many years: a unique collection of documents, records and letters from the beginning of Zionism as a national movement onwards.

On 30 January 1933, the day Hitler was named Chancellor of Germany, Herlitz immediately determined to transfer the entire archive from Meinekestraße in Berlin's Wilmersdorf district to Jerusalem. He followed the advice of his wife on the matter and, rather than trying to spirit the archival materials out of the country at the dead of night, registered his plan with the police in line with regulations. 'My wife justified her suggestion on the grounds that the Prussians, even after the National Socialists had come to power, would surely remain correct officials.'

And so it proved: the police captain to whom Herlitz had presented his request thanked him for his trust, asked for the relevant submissions, and promised the stunned petitioner that he would not let him down and that nothing bad would happen to his collections. 'From 15 September 1933 onwards a lorry appeared punctually every morning in front of the office building at 10 Meinekestraße, delivered ten empty, seaworthy crates and picked up the ten crates delivered the previous day, now packed with material. This continued for fifteen days, until a total of 154 crates had been transported away and the rooms of the Zionist Archives were empty. We left nothing behind in Berlin, not a document nor a book, nor a photo, nor a map, not even the smallest slip of paper of any documentary significance.'

Rehavia was this as well: a city of officials in the Prussian mould.

Gingeria

Yehuda Haezrahi called his novel of his childhood, published in 1968, *Ir, even ve-Shamayim* ('City of Stone and Sky'). Formed from memories of a childhood in Rehavia, it reaches back to the time the neighbourhood came into being in the 1920s. The area was originally called 'Gingeria', on account of the hue of its rock, from which the unmistakeable honey-coloured stone of the city was quarried. Arthur Ruppin described the hilly terrain around the Old City:

> In the distance you can see the Old City, encircled by the city wall. Outside of the Old City, Jerusalem at that time was an assemblage of just a few streets and a handful of settlements scattered across the hills. There were the bustling markets by Jaffa Gate and Damascus Gate, the wretched shops along the cobbled pavements of Jaffa Street with the dusty, not yet surfaced road in between, the Mea Shearim

neighbourhood, the streets of Bukharan, Yemin Moshe and Nahalat Shiva, all of them densely built, one house on top of another, and inward-looking, like isolated citadels – yes, citadels of the poor – surrounded by the desert, and the monasteries, most of them high up in the mountains, with their courtyards enclosed with walls and entrances secured by heavy iron doors. Every morning and evening their clocks rang out, one clock tower called and in the distance another answered. But the Zionists who came here saw in their peculiar dreams of the New Jerusalem the green meadows and woods of their European homelands. They wanted to build a city and live in nature at the same time. They wanted to build settlements of little stone houses with red-tiled roofs and a grove of trees and a garden around every house and quiet streets leading often to squares, avenues, and parks. A munificent and prettily coloured vision, to beautify the sacredness of ancient Jerusalem.

On Shabbat morning the parents set out with their children for a picnic on a rocky plot of land. The father is in a pale summer suit, straw hat and tie with a walking stick in his hand; the mother wears a bright dress with lace collar; one son sports a bow tie and the other a sailor suit. The parents point to an area of stone: 'We're going to build a house here.' They indicate where the staircase, the hallway, the garden will be, and in the sky where the large balcony will go, and where the small. A house made of pure breeze, Shabbat, stone and sky. A half dozen houses around it. The judge Gad Frumkin has built one out of elegant white stone with the word 'Hahavatselet' ('Lily') engraved in the middle of the entranceway. Others include the then president, Yitzhak Ben-Zvi's, symbolically humble wooden hut and the proud house of Arthur Ruppin.

To the child Yehuda Haezrahi, the neighbourhood Richard Kauffmann planned seemed entirely symmetrical:

> You could draw Rehavia seen from the air as the upper half of a man's body. The Hebrew Gymnasium building is the head. Keren Kayemet Le-Israel looks like the shoulders and arms, spread out in both directions. Ibn Gabirol and Ibn Ezra Streets lead southwards, not straight but on a slant, towards the narrow hips. In the middle, the imaginary spine: a garden stretches out alongside Yehuda Halevi Avenue (called Kuzari Avenue today for some inscrutable reason). Every house is inscribed within this formal and symmetrical figure; every house is surrounded by a garden which is twice the size of the house. Just so and not otherwise.

Haezrahi, born in 1920, witnessed how Rehavia turned from a dreamed-of garden city into reality. He characterised it exactly:

> Garden city? A settlement of cottages surrounded by trees and flowerbeds, far removed from the uproar of the city? Not quite. The years passed and it became apparent that Rehavia did not lie outside the city centre, but rather almost was the centre. The small houses gained an extra storey or two. Many were torn down. Lumpen housing blocks were built in their place, with no space for their own garden. Property owners in settlements like that don't look

after the flowerbeds anyway. The streets, deliberately laid out narrow and conceived for a low volume of traffic, are suddenly filled with lorries, buses and cars with stinking exhausts. Before Rehavia's developers could take a second look, this future had already arrived.

Rehavia shares this fate with other garden cities, where green ideas have ground to a halt in black asphalt and gridlock. From its beginning, the idea of the garden city in its German form concealed within it a strongly ideological element. One of its originators, Theodor Fritsch, proselytised for it on antisemitic grounds: that nature and countryside were antithetical to the Jews, who were thought of as living in the big cities, far away from any natural element – another stereotype confounded by Rehavia.

'Rehavia stays German!'

Like all of Israel, Rehavia was a land of many languages; fundamentally, it still is today. While the chief language of this Jerusalem neighbourhood was German, the status of that language changed over the years. In 1933 and 1934, Esther Herlitz and her girlfriends were teased on account of their mother tongue; a few years earlier they would have been spared that – or at least not had the curse 'Nazi' spat at them. David Kroyanker, who himself grew up there in the 1930s and 1940s, remembered 'Rehavia stays German!' being the area's slogan.

Hebrew was the language of the Yishuv, but immigrants mastered it to varying degrees, a section of them not at all. The 'ulpanim', high quality Hebrew classes to help immigrants from different countries integrate, did not yet exist. The older generation often came to grief in their acquisition of the language.

In autumn 1933, Georg Herlitz arrived by boat in Haifa and took the bus to Jerusalem. Almost every passenger was speaking Yiddish. Suddenly the bus came to a halt. After some time, another bus stopped on the opposite side of the road; its driver disembarked and advised his clueless colleague in Yiddish: 'Gib a Klapp auf die Klatsch!' ('Press down on the clutch!') The spluttering bus only actually got moving again by using reverse. But Herlitz had his first lesson in the most widely spoken language of his new homeland.

He wrote about his struggles to learn Hebrew. Once when he was laboriously searching for words, a colleague addressed him in Yiddish. A supervisor heard this as he walked past, stopped and summoned Herlitz to his office: 'It is forbidden to speak a language other than Hebrew to anyone in the office.'

German became more and more a private language. After 1933 it vanished entirely from school curricula.

Arthur Ruppin, who learned Hebrew early, recounts a wedding in Jerusalem in November 1936:

Big dinner, fifty guests, eating for five hours, fifteen speakers [...] In my speech in Hebrew I supplied the hit of the evening, when I said of Mrs Lili Schocken: "Hageveret Hashohehvet al yadi" instead of "hayosvet". (The lady, who is "lying" next to me, instead of "sitting".) Great hilarity. But I resolved to give no more after-dinner speeches in Hebrew.

Even Gershom Scholem, who achieved virtuoso mastery in Hebrew, writes that he was nervous of practising his profession as a maths teacher in Jerusalem and only did so for a short time, out of fear that the children would make fun of his Berlin accent, which made the Hebrew letter 'resh' close to inaudible.

Gad Granach's mother lived over thirty-eight years in Israel and knew just one word of Hebrew: 'mishpaha'.

When she turned eighty, she moved into an old people's home. Whenever I visited her there she wanted to let the old people sat around her know that I was her son. So every time she pointed her finger at me and said: "Mishpaha, mishpaha!", while stubbornly emphasising the wrong syllable, that is, the second instead of the last. But my mother got along astonishingly well without Hebrew: she simply spoke German to everyone, very loudly at that, and everyone soon understood her.

Mrs Granach acquired instead a basic knowledge of Yiddish by listening night after night to the news at seven o'clock, read by Reuven Rubinstein. It sounded something like this: 'A giten Obend und a giten Schabbes, meine lieben Zuherer und Zuhererinnen ...' – 'Good evening and a good Shabbat, my dear listeners. First the news, read by Ruwen Rubinstein: Arab murderers have been attacking across the border. They fired their weapons, including shooting at Yiddish farmworkers. But Yiddish blood will not be shed for nothing. The Yiddish soldiers were not alarmed. These enemies of Israel were repelled and beaten up. Shabbat shalom!'

Great tragedies and troubles have a different ring in Yiddish. But in spite of, or precisely because of, all the anecdotes one must not lose sight of how essential this question of language was. An inadequate grasp of Hebrew led almost always to exclusion and isolation, and brought derision and scepticism in its wake. At every stage of our tour of Rehavia we will be faced with this shibboleth for entry into Jewish society. The language question poses itself anew in every decade: in the 1930s it is decidedly different from a decade earlier. In his novel *De Vriendt Goes Home* Arnold Zweig writes about the languages of Jerusalem at the end of the 1920s:

> In Jerusalem three languages rule: English, spoken by tourists, officials and those natives who want to get information out of them quickly; Hebrew, for Jews communicating among themselves, especially the younger ones, on the street, everywhere in public life; and among the non-Jews, however, in general, Arabic.

Synagogues in Rehavia

A fair amount has been published in German on the immigration of German Jews to Palestine, but on Rehavia in particular there is only one book, one excellent book: *Ashkenazi in Jerusalem*, the doctoral thesis of Christian Kraft, published in 2014, on 'The Religious Institutions of Immigrants from Germany in the Rehavia District of Jerusalem (1933–2004) – Transfer and Transformation'. Kraft asks what traditions of their religious, communal life Jews from Germany, both Orthodox and Reform, brought with them and what became of those traditions in their new environment over the years that followed. It is a fascinating enquiry: to what extent did the religious institutions resist change in a place as secular as Rehavia? How were these institutions constituted? Did they separate themselves from the rest or integrate?

Though the Great Synagogue stands not far from Rehavia, you should not imagine that the synagogues which came after it were magnificent buildings, expansively laid out, with richly furnished interiors. They were makeshift and modest sacred shelters. In this context, 'Ashkenazi' means German. From 1937 onwards, Orthodox immigrants newly arrived from Germany – in Hebrew all Jewish immigrants to Israel are called 'olim', the 'ascending' – met up regularly in Rehavia to worship according to the southern Ashkenazi rite, a variant of the rite in the synagogues of south Germany. Because this small congregation had in the beginning no fixed abode, services took place in various different flats and houses in Rehavia. From February 1940, Rabbi Unna, born in Würzburg in 1872, rented a flat at 18 Menahem Ussishkin Street, which remained a meeting place for the 'Binyan Zion' ('House of Zion') congregation for over sixty years, until 2004. This group took its name from an old religious text and at the same time gestured into the future, linking obedience to the law with the establishment of a new polity: Zion understood both biblically and politically.

In this small congregation, the Torah and Talmud were taught, lectures on both arts and sciences were given, themes from the philosophy of religion were discussed and disseminated in letters to the congregation, printed or typed on a typewriter.

A Jewish joke tells of two shipwrecked Jews who take refuge on a life-sustaining but unpopulated island. When they are eventually located, their rescuers discover two synagogues at opposite ends of the island, built from the meagre supply of wood. In answer to the amazed question, why the two of them did not share one synagogue, comes from two mouths one unanimous answer: so that the one should not have to step foot in the other's building.

In the same year that Binyan Zion was founded, men from three German-speaking Orthodox prayer groups established the Horeb Synagogue on the neighbouring Ibn Gabirol Street, named for the chief pedagogical text of Samson Raphael Hirsch, the founder of 'neo-Orthodoxy' in Germany in the nineteenth century. Horeb held separate services and, with its Orthodox youth group and its school of the same name, had a different ideological orientation from Binyan Zion. Half of its pupils were from Germany and were rigorously selected on the basis of their parents' fidelity to the Torah.

Jerusalem's garden city therefore drew pious families as well as secular ones. The historian Mordechai Breuer (1918–2007), from Frankfurt am Main, son of Isaac Breuer, co-founder of the Horeb Synagogue, explained why in an interview:

So, we came here at the beginning of March 1936. And already within two or three months my mother had rented a flat for us in Rehavia. Why Rehavia? When we arrived in '36, there were perhaps two or three synagogues in Rehavia, including a private synagogue. So Rehavia didn't have an Orthodox or a religious image. But near to Rehavia, right next to it, Sha'arei Hesed is an old-Orthodox neighbourhood. The question is, why did my parents and very many other Orthodox Jews choose precisely this neighbourhood, Rehavia? [...] The choice of Rehavia may perhaps be typical of this group. Which says something about the particular nature of neo-Orthodoxy. It's not a simple return to Orthodoxy, bypassing the Reform after the eighteenth century. That was gone. For new or neo-Orthodoxy, the Judaism of the Ghetto was not the ideal.

A synthesis of modernity and Orthodoxy emerged in Rehavia, a compound of a secular way of life with obedience to the law, under the Rabbinical phrase that Hirsch had put at the centre of neo-Orthodoxy, 'Torah im Derech Eretz', that is, combining fidelity to the Torah with the worldly laws of the land. A Reform congregation developed too: Emet v'Emunah ('Truth and Faith').

After joint studies in history and Jewish theology in Breslau and a doctorate in Würzburg, Rabbi Kurt Wilhelm (1900–1965) studied in New York, qualifying as a rabbi at the Jewish Theological Seminary there and subsequently serving as a rabbi in Braunschweig and Dortmund. A Zionist thinker in an anti-Zionist environment, Wilhelm emigrated to Jerusalem in autumn 1933 and set up his own congregation soon after. In 1940 it obtained its present-day premises in Gan Rehavia. From the beginning Wilhelm developed an educational programme; his place of worship was at the same time a 'cultural centre in the spirit of Jewish congregations in Germany', as Michael Shashar writes.

Shmuel Hugo Bergmann recalls his first encounter with the young rabbi from Germany, in the summer of 1936, when

Wilhelm was propounding his ideas for the establishment of a 'German' religious community:

> The old familiar tunes need to be renewed. The chief weight should fall on preaching. Hebrew studies should begin and German continue. In fact learning must stand at the very centre of the synagogue's work. The Bat Mitzvah [the ceremony of religious majority for girls] must be introduced alongside the Bar Mitzvah [the ceremony for boys]. We must make contact with areligious groups. We must travel across the country with the Bible. Above all what is lacking is proper ministry.

Wilhelm, working with Georg Herlitz and Moritz Kalvaryski, began drafting their reform programme in German. In Hebrew they framed the grounding principles of liberal Judaism far more strictly, in order to win the approval of the Orthodox Chief Rabbinate of Eretz Israel. As a result, Kook, the Ashkenazi Chief Rabbi, granted Rabbi Wilhelm the right to conduct marriages in his congregation. With this the congregation began to draw in young people as well from the surrounding area.

One member of the congregation remembers how Wilhelm led a Tikkun (a liturgy) every year on the night of Shavuot (the Feast of Weeks) in Café Tuv Taam in Rehavia. In line with the traditional commandment, the café was decked with fresh greenery in honour of the occasion:

> Those present at the "Tikkun" were for the most part from the "new Aliyah" at that time, immigrants from Ashkenazi

lands, who had come to the country under duress and were oppressed by their material impoverishment and still more by their Jewish-spiritual impoverishment. But they thirsted after a Jewish and a Hebrew renewal. The young rabbi was able to quench that thirst. He understood how to give that mysterious rite of "Tikkun Lail ha-Shavuot" a new content, which originated in the Kabbalist circles of Safed in Israel. That night was unforgettable for all who were there – in a friendly, pleasant atmosphere, eating cheesecake [the traditional dish of the festival] and studying Torah together, even though some of the students were such deep-thinking, sage personalities as Martin Buber (who, for the sake of his friend, Rav Wilhelm, was prepared to put his scepticism towards organised religion to one side)…

The German-Jewish congregations in Rehavia established their own educational institutions in the tradition of the Jewish 'study house'. In this, Emet v'Emunah – unlike Horeb and Binyan Zion – went well beyond tuition in Jewish doctrine. In partnership with the Association of Immigrants from Germany and Austria, formed in 1938 as a result of the great number of refugees, and the equivalent association for immigrants from Czechoslovakia, Emet v'Emunah offered not only Hebrew lessons but also seminars on Judaism and Palestine conducted in German, and the congregation offered professional training courses as well. In the winter term Martin Buber gave a lecture on the fundamental doctrines of Hasidism and the following winter one on 'Judaism/Christianity'. The educator Ernst Simon, the philosopher Shmuel Hugo Bergmann and the orientalist Dov Goitein spoke on their specialist fields, as did Gershom Scholem and Julius Guttmann. The historian Richard Koebner even gave talks in their home community Rehavia. There were scholars of non-German origin as well, such as the Bible scholar Moshe David Cassuto and the biologist and religious thinker Yeshayahu Leibowitz.

In 1944, the teaching programme for the Binyan Zion synagogue offered a lecture series on England. Notable members of the congregation spoke on English society, English law, English literature, London's (Jewish) East End, 'English Statesmen in the Middle East' and 'Shakespeare and the Jews (the Shylock Problem)'. They were getting closer to the Mandatory Power.

Kurt Wilhelm, however, left Jerusalem soon after the foundation of the state of Israel and in 1948 became Chief Rabbi in Stockholm, a shock for his congregation and for Rehavia. Many saw him from then on as a 'Yored', the Hebrew name for the 'descending' emigrant from Israel, as opposed to the 'ascending' immigrant. But German Jewry did not let go of Wilhelm even in Stockholm. He encountered the German-born Nobel Prize winner Nelly Sachs there and had a great influence on her writing. Shortly before his death in 1965, Wilhelm returned to Jerusalem.

The Yeshurun Synagogue was built between 1934 and 1936 on the edge of Rehavia. It was an American-Jewish project for a modern Orthodox congregation, supported by Judah Leon Magnes, chancellor and later president of the Hebrew University; the judge Gad Frumkin; the lawyer Mordecai Eliash; and Hannah (Annie) Landau, headmistress of the Rothschild School – all of whom wanted to become members of this new congregation. By 1936 the money was running out and there were fears that construction would not be completed. But then a wealthy, unattached lady from Cape Town made a substantial donation for the 'synagogue in the Holy City'. The work was completed. The building was designed by architects Meir Rubin and Alexander Friedmann in the International Style, like other national institutions, with a curved front, flowing in the Bauhaus style, with narrow vertical windows in a plain façade. The Yeshurun Society had bought the plot of land from the Ratisbonne Monastery. At first there were worries that the monastery's illuminated cross would, from a certain perspective, cast light on the roof of the synagogue as well. But the location of the plot, right next to Rehavia, proved itself advantageous.

In the early summer of 1939 Yechiel Michel Schlesinger founded the Kol Torah ('Voice of the Torah') yeshiva – a Jewish religious academy – in Rehavia in partnership with Baruch Kunstadt and a small circle of Orthodox Jews. On 25 June 1939, sixteen bahurim ('young men' but also 'Torah students') were students at the yeshiva; half a year later the enrolment had doubled. Schlesinger was among the Talmidei Hachamim ('learned students') who had brought their profound Talmudic education from Lithuania to Germany, and from there to Rehavia.

Yechiel Michel Schlesinger was born in Hamburg in 1898, the son of Rabbi Eliezer Lipmann Schlesinger and his wife, Sarah. While still a child, he received instruction at home, attending Hamburg's Talmud-Torah School while also being taught the Talmud and Torah by the Hungarian-born Rabbi Abraham Samuel Spitzer. It was presumably on Spitzer's recommendation that he went to Hungary during the First

World War, in order to study at the German-language yeshiva in Galanta. The outstanding scholar returned to Germany in 1921 and studied at the Orthodox rabbinic seminary in Berlin at the same time as working on a doctorate in Oriental Studies. In 1928, having completed his doctoral thesis on Aramaic syntax in the Talmud, he sent a brief telegram to his parents in Hamburg: 'A man free, to study Torah.'

Here was the proud slogan of a young Jew who had dedicated the rest of his life to Torah study. He travelled to Lithuania to further his learning and four years later took on a job at the Breuer yeshiva in Frankfurt am Main. On the morning of 10 November 1938 he narrowly escaped arrest and made it to Palestine via Switzerland with his family.

Schlesinger died in 1949, ten years after founding the Kol Torah yeshiva, and was survived by his mother in Jerusalem and his wife, Matte, a native of Frankfurt, who died in 2001 aged ninety-seven.

Orthodoxy found its place in Rehavia, though the neighbourhood's religious life was in many ways a reflection of its secular: pragmatic, open, dialogical, bilingual, inclusive not exclusive, fostering education and putting work at the heart of things. The founding rabbi of Binyan Zion wrote: 'Young people of the wider community have been brought up with a single ideal, "work". [...] But work alone cannot fulfil a person, cannot satisfy his spirit; after six days the sabbath must come, the day of rest, of elevating the mind and spirit.'

The 'German form of worship' was understood to include particular practices: an ordained solemn prayer for festivals, fixed times for prayer, a separate women's section in the synagogue and a sermon on the sabbath. More than once, members of the congregations of Binyan Zion and Horeb aspired to a merger; their attempts foundered on differences in ritual. Yitzhak Weill, board member of Binyan Zion, born in Frankfurt am Main, remembered later:

> We preserved the legacy of the synagogues in Germany, the *Rites in Full*, comprising 'Bless my Lord, O my soul' [psalm 104] as well as 'And I gave you' [First Book of Moses 1:29, part of the Havdalah ritual to end Shabbat], from the selichot [penitential prayers on Yom Kippur] and the piyyutim [liturgical poems] and a particular melody for every occasion.

In fact the Horeb congregation, like Binyan Zion, swiftly gave up the German-Ashkenazi rite for a Jerusalemite one, though there was no necessity to do so in Jewish tradition. But, as Christian Kraft shows, we may presume that this was the German-Jewish congregations integrating themselves into the majority society, making accommodations with a changed environment, without giving up their distinct traditions, which should continue to be vital into the next century.

The Taste of Rehavia

What did Rehavia taste of? How were things cooked? What kind of restaurants were there – if there were restaurants at all? What sort of cafés? What influence did the warm climate have on the cuisine? Which traditions from Germany survived; which came to an end? What was on sale in the shops?

In her reportage from Rehavia, Gabriele Tergit reminds us that two-thirds of Jerusalem contained dreadful slum housing:

... built out of sheet metal from petrol cans, laths and roofing felt, offering little protection from the heat or the awful winter cold. Unsurfaced roads full of rubbish, orange skins and rags. And next to them are friendly, petit bourgeois areas, houses with smooth fronts and large covered terraces behind.

And then there was Rehavia.

Alisa Eshad's 2013 documentary film *Quatsch mit Soße* ('Nonsense with Sauce' – the title is a pun on a German expression meaning 'total nonsense') seeks out the eating habits and dishes of the Yekkes in Israel, and with that the eating habits and cooking of Israel as a whole. The Yekkes interviewed in the film, mostly from Rehavia, remember their mothers' cooking, or in one case their father's. Avraham Frank condenses his culinary memories into a single phrase: the food at home was spartan. Naomi Abele counts at most five spices in use in her home. Batya and Gadi Ackerman recall spinach served with a fried egg and fried potatoes. Masha Cohen describes 'Heaven and Earth' – a Silesian dish made of apples (the heaven) and potatoes (the earth) – as a punishment. The culinary high points, according to Naomi Ehrlich-Kuperman, are the Würstchen (little sausages) with mustard and the potato salad. For Dena Greenspan, precisely this salad seems the quintessential yekkish dish.

Avraham Frank explains how every Jewish household, whether Orthodox or liberal, strictly kosher or not kosher, has a large cast iron pot with two handles, in which the 'cholent', the traditional Jewish dish for Shabbat, is prepared with beans, duck meat and potatoes. The devout families carry the pot on

Friday to the local baker, who keeps it warm in his oven. At midday on Shabbat the pot is fetched and then carried back there after the meal.

Gadi Yakov shows us the compact kitchen in a yekkish house: the small kitchen cabinet with fold-out sideboard and integrated shelving, the first pressure cooker.

The grapefruit arrived from the orchard into the closed world of German cooking, halved and separated into slices with some jam in the middle. The fruit on offer was different from in central Europe. There were oranges, lemons, bananas, the new persimmons and, early in the year, strawberries, but hardly any raspberries, currants or other fruits which needed more water and could not tolerate too much heat. There were trusted types of vegetable, such as tomatoes, cucumbers and cauliflower, but hardly any winter cabbage or turnip. In their place: aubergines and avocados.

The film shows fine table napkins with embroidered monograms, and ivory spoons for boiled eggs – silver would have discoloured – and all recall the importance of table manners in their upbringing. On the meticulously laid table stand Meissen porcelain and china bought from Rosenthal or KPM in Berlin.

Yonathan Livni shows how to prepare red cabbage with onions and 'white meat' – the circumlocution for 'pork', in this case, bacon.

There was often tongue, which has a firm place in kosher cuisine, but also roast goose, stuffed beef brisket and hash of calf's lights. Henny Kneller shows how to mould and bake a meatloaf. Kikoe Epstein prepares the traditional matzo dumplings from matzo flour, parsley and onion. Her husband, Uri Epstein, remembers meanwhile the regional diversity of

German cooking, the east and west, north and south. From southern Germany comes the thick 'bean soup', in reality a hotpot with a great deal of meat.

Tomer Kaufman has bought chicken breasts from Mahane Yehuda, the Jewish market in Jerusalem. He hammers them flat, turns them in egg yolk and breadcrumbs and fries them: Wiener Schnitzel, which he serves in his small Jerusalem restaurant.

Another interviewee in the film, Ilan Oppenheimer, describes the taste of his first whipped cream – from the Garden of Eden. Uriel Adiv shows his grandmother Resi Gumpel's handwritten and precisely dated recipe book. Even the preparation of jam and marmalade found a way into the Israeli kitchen as part of German cookery.

To what in Israel today would be an obvious question about 'Middle Eastern food', an older married couple from Rehavia answers: 'Certainly not!' Jewish and Arab cuisines were indeed for a long time rigorously separated. Residents of Rehavia went 'to the Arab' in the old city and encountered what today would count as signature elements of Israeli cuisine: tahini, hummus, aubergines, labneh, oriental spices, the traditional parsley salad, lamb, chicken and grilled fish. The eastern Jewish merchants stocked gherkins, cabbage and dill.

One older lady explains: 'Western Jews – no garlic. Those from the east, absolutely. And as a result, they stink.' This cultivated arrogance was not confined to the dividing line of western and eastern Jewish cuisine.

And towards the end of the film the viewer sees the rich variety of German baking: Black Forest cherry or chocolate cake, Kringel (a kind of sweet pretzel), Königskuchen (fruit cakes) and biscuits.

In the face of these culinary riches one should not forget the serious shortages in Israel both during and after the foundation of the state: when Jerusalem was under siege in the early summer of 1948 there was pretty much nothing to buy; even water was rationed. And in the early 1950s foodstuffs were so scarce that ration cards had to be issued. In the young nation, luxury remained a taboo. There were fruit and vegetables from the market and small shops in neighbourhoods, for the most part run by eastern Jews. And there was the 'Mittagstisch' ('lunch table'), a now-forgotten arrangement that had existed previously in Germany: unattached workers, mostly men, eating at lunchtime in a private household. The family table expanded to include paying guests. The philosopher Hans Jonas, who in the thirties was a subletter with the dentist Dr Erlanger and his wife, joined a 'lunch table' at the Hagelberg boarding house.

Amos Oz remembered the taste of his childhood:

We had an iron rule that one should never buy anything imported, anything foreign, if it was possible to buy a locally-made equivalent. Still, when we went to Mr Auster's grocery shop, on the corner of Obadiah and Amos Streets, we had to choose between kibbutz cheese, made by the Jewish co-operative Tnuva, and Arab cheese: did Arab cheese from the nearby village, Lifta, count as home-made or imported produce? Tricky. True, the Arab cheese was just a little bit cheaper. But if you bought Arab cheese, weren't you being a traitor to Zionism? Somewhere, in some kibbutz or moshav, in the Jezreel Valley or the hills of Galilee, an overworked pioneer girl was sitting, with tears in her eyes perhaps, packing this Hebrew cheese for us – how could we turn our backs on her and buy alien cheese? Did we have the heart? On the other hand, if we boycotted the produce of our Arab neighbours, we would be deepening and perpetuating the hatred between our two peoples. And we would be partly responsible for any blood that was shed, heaven forbid. Surely the humble Arab *fellah*, a simple, honest tiller of the soil, whose soul was still undefiled by the miasma of town life, was nothing more nor less than the dusky brother of the simple, noble-hearted *mujik* in the stories of Tolstoy! Could we be so heartless as to turn our backs on this rustic cheese? Could we be so cruel as to punish him? What for? Because the deceitful British and the corrupt effendis had set him against us. No. This time we would definitely buy the cheese from the Arab village, which incidentally really did taste better than the Tnuva cheese, and cost a little less into the bargain. But still, on the third hand, what if the Arab cheese wasn't too clean? Who knew what the dairies were like there? What if it turned out, too late, that their cheese was full of germs?

Upon these bacilli Oz's grandmother Shlomit had declared war. 'The Levant is full of microbes!' was the battle cry of her cleaning, which no doubt also had to do with the early immigrants' experiences of malaria and yellow fever and with the initially inadequate sewer system and often unclean water in Jerusalem. Gershom Scholem wrote that for two years after his arrival in 1923 he drank only boiled water and slept under a mosquito net.

During the Mandatory Period, the small city centre was

primarily Ben Yehuda Street, with its shops and cafés, divided up by nationality:

The Hungarians sat apart and the Yekkes sat apart and the Polish Jews sat somewhere else again. Wherever it smelt of food, that's where the Hungarians were. There were magazines in the cafés. You could sit with a cup of coffee for four or five hours and read magazines. There were big beautiful portfolios containing at minimum ten different illustrated magazines, exactly like the "reading circles" in Germany. Something the Yekkes had introduced here. There was a war on of course, but the magazines arrived from everywhere: the *Neue Zürcher Zeitung*, the *Zürcher Illustrierte*, the *Schweizer Illustrierte*. Some even came from Germany. The English magazines, which always had the latest news about the royal household on their first pages, were particularly coveted.

So Gad Granach reminisces and reels off the cafés: Café Alaska with its pretty waitresses, most of them recent arrivals from Germany; Café Sichel with its large garden and mixed clientele, including oriental Jews; Café Vienna with its well-heeled Arabs; genteel Café Europa with its waiters in black suit and bow tie and frescoes of the cities of Palestine by the artist Jakob Steinhardt.

Later in the evening people went to Fink's Bar, a West Jerusalem institution, well stocked with journalists and foreign correspondents. Winston Churchill had once sat there too. One thoroughly yekkish spot in Rehavia was the Vienna Tea Room: there 'the better type of English sat and drank tea from small warmed pots, always pouring in the milk before the tea so as not to discolour the cups. The cakes in the Vienna Tea Room were wonderful and people spoke German or English.'

Young Granach had strawberries and whipped cream in the colony established not far from Rehavia by the German Templers. In 1941 the British Mandatory Powers interned the often Nazi-inclined Templers. Granach has an untamed, irreverent spirit: he looks at Rehavia with a dash of irony and a trace of mistrust, caused by so much German culture. He remembers:

> The Yekkes opened one delicatessen after another on Ben Yehuda Street and Jaffa Street. One was called Sternschuss, one Levy and one Futter, which was the best. None were kosher. At Futter only German was spoken and everything was done with a decided sophistication. Herr Futter was as rotten as the night and Frau Futter was a beauty. How the two got together, I do not know, but they had marvellous ham, which they were able to slice very thinly, and they addressed every customer by name. Apparently, the ham came from Nazareth, where the Christian Arabs raised pigs.

In his talk on 'Lübeck as a Way of Life and Thought', Thomas Mann refers to the fact that 'the Orient is involved' in the origins of marzipan. Its recipe and ingredients came 'from the lands of the Orient via Venice to Lübeck'. One has before one, he says, a 'harem confectionery'. And yet at the same time marzipan was the epitome of that bourgeois German world Walter Benjamin described in his *Berlin Childhood around 1900*.

Franziska Baruch was born in 1901 into a not-quite-middle-class Jewish family in the neighbouring city of Hamburg. From 1919 to 1925 she studied graphic and book design in the educational institute of the Prussian Museum of Applied Arts in Berlin and brought a multifaceted talent and practical mindset to work for widely varying clients. In 1921 she designed the text for a book-lover's Pesach-Haggadah (the order for the Passover Seder) with woodcuts by Jakob Steinhardt, who would later produce the frescoes in Jerusalem's Café Europa. And in 1928, still not yet twenty-seven years old, Baruch was commissioned by Junior Arts Minister Edwin Redslob to design the government's promotional campaign for the international 'Pressa' exhibition in Cologne. Alongside this, she was developing Hebrew fonts. For the publisher Salman Schocken, the young typographer designed the cover for the Hebrew edition of the tales of S.Y. Agnon. In her professional life she was at home in both languages.

In 1933 Baruch emigrated to Palestine. The few graphic commissions she accepted there weren't enough for her to live on. Necessity made her ingenious. When the supply of goods from Germany came to an end with the outbreak of war in 1939, no more marzipan could make it to the holy city. But the Arab merchants had almonds, pistachios, sesame seeds and rose water. To this day no one has got hold of the company Niederegger's secret recipe, closely guarded in Lübeck since the nineteenth century. But you could make marzipan from what was on offer at the oriental market. Baruch, penniless and unemployed, found the ingredients in Jerusalem's Old City and baked marzipan.

In 1943 the confectioner-cum-designer designed packaging

for her product that must have seemed familiar to all the afi-
cionados of marzipan in that distant place. She emulated the
packaging that Alfred Mahlau had designed in Lübeck
in the 1920s and which to this day is a trademark of the Niederegger company. Jerusalem replaced Lübeck; the walls and
battlements of the Old City took the place of the Holsten Gate
and silhouette of that once proud Hanseatic city, by then long
since mired in National Socialism. Mahlau had long before
proffered his services to the regime and Niederegger's marzipan factory had been destroyed in a devastating air raid in
March 1942. German lettering became Hebrew. The inscrip-
tion bearing greetings from Lübeck was replaced with greetings
from Jerusalem; Christmas wishes in German were replaced
with English. No doubt 'Baruch's biscuits' tasted different to
the Lübeck marzipan. In its presentation it adopted a design
that was familiar and yet at the same time new. Even this marzipan and its packaging bears witness from 1943 to a destruction
and transformation that spared nothing and no one.

Life Stories of a Neighbourhood

Kabbalist: Gershom Scholem

Gershom Scholem's Hebrew bears the same unmistakeable Berlin tinge as his German. He wrote his autobiography in both languages, first in German in 1977 as *From Berlin to Jerusalem*, then four years later in Hebrew as *Mi-Berlin li-Yerushalayim*. His Berlin cadences pervade both versions.

At the end of his long life, Gerhard – who adopted the name Gershom as a young man – Scholem returned a final time to his birthplace and in December 1981 presented his reminiscences in the grand hall of the Jewish Community Centre on Fasanenstraße. There was no shortage of similar memories from the pens of Berliner children:

> But what is perhaps peculiar in my case, is that I want to speak of the life of a young Jew, whose path led from the Berlin of my childhood and youth to Jerusalem and Israel. To me this path seemed peculiarly direct and clearly signposted; to others – my own family included – it seemed unfathomable, not to say enraging.

The Hebrew version of his memoirs, published in 1982, was Scholem's last authorised book. It was a legacy of his beginnings, written in his life's two languages, but in the latter version expanded and modified, because Scholem wanted to give an Israeli readership a more detailed picture of the history of early Zionism, his immigration in 1923 and above all his first two years in Jerusalem.

In the autumn of 1923, as the twenty-five-year-old's boat docked in Jaffa a day late – Scholem cited Arthur Holitscher's travelogue saying that the cliffs of Jaffa were no metaphor – he had almost reached his longed-for goal on Yom Kippur, the highest of the Jewish holy days. After an immigration procedure lasting several hours, his fiancée Escha picked him up at the harbour. They travelled by horse-drawn carriage to Tel Aviv, where the two of them wandered the city absorbed in endless looking and conversation. On 30 September 1923 the pair arrived with their suitcases in Jerusalem by lorry. They lived with friends at first, then moved into the Bukharan Quarter near to Mea Shearim, one of Jerusalem's Orthodox neighbourhoods. Then in 1932 to Rehavia.

When Scholem, in his eightieth year, wrote his memoirs, he was able to draw on his many letters from his mother, which spanned from the time of the First World War through to 1946:

She was a born journalist, exceptionally nimble and apt in expression, and in a time when women were not yet allowed near such a profession, had doubtless as a result missed out on her proper vocation, in which she would have been a dazzling part of the editorial team at Ullstein. She wrote letters in the grand style, long feuilletons often, and by the way in a girl's calligraphic script – I have saved several bundles of her later letters to Jerusalem.

The correspondence between mother and son was published seven years after Scholem's death.

Betty Scholem was the balancing, conciliating counterpart to Gershom's father. The son recalls how his mother presented opposite views on the same subject in different company. When he criticised her for this, his mother responded, 'My son, don't find fault with me.' Only later did he realise the many strains his mother had withstood and counterbalanced. Arthur Scholem, proprietor of a printing firm in Berlin's Mitte district, belonged in habits and mindset entirely to the assimilated middling Jewish bourgeoisie of the time of the Kaiser, who had achieved some prosperity by dint of hard work. A man of choleric temper, Arthur expelled his son from the family home in 1917. (It was around this time that Scholem adopted the Biblical Hebrew name 'Gershom' as an alternative to the Germanic 'Gerhard' he had been given at birth.)

The four sons of Arthur and Betty Scholem, born at two-year intervals – 1891, 1893, 1895 and 1897 – stand for four paths of German Jewry in that period: the oldest, Reinhold, for the German nationalist path, a political orientation he maintained over decades in Australian exile and into old age; the second, Erich, for the path of bourgeois assimilation; and the third, Werner, a gifted speaker who later became a Reichstag deputy for the German Communist Party (KPD), for the path of political action. Gerhard dedicated his memoirs of his youth to Werner, who was closest to him among his brothers and who was murdered in Buchenwald concentration camp in 1940. And finally Gerhard, the youngest, with his rapidly crystallising path through life, embodies the ethos of early Zionism: returning to and reappropriating one's history by emigrating.

Scholem strongly understood his early years in Berlin, and still more his years as a student in Jena and Munich and his time in Switzerland and Heidelberg, as a preparation for the land of Israel, for Jerusalem. In his last years, his origins in Berlin returned in powerful, glowing colours.

In the Rehavia directory of 1936 Gershom Scholem had himself listed as a 'Kabbalist', surely a job title unique in the world, in the sense of a civilian profession, not an inner calling. It signified not the practice of the Kabbalah, an esoteric tradition within Jewish mysticism, but research into manuscripts, tracts, letters and books: the Kabbalist as philologist. Scholem discovered the Kabbalah as early as 1915, when he was graduating from secondary school, and with it the theme of his life and the foundation for his own new subject in Jerusalem.

Two years after he emigrated, Scholem became a lecturer at the newly opened Hebrew University. In the summer of 1925, he announced to the Hebrew poet Hayim Nahman Bialik the project that would occupy him for nearly six decades:

> Until today, nothing has been done towards scholarly research of the Kabbalah. This, nevertheless, is the hoped-for and struggle-worthy objective of such research: to learn and write the history of the evolution of the Kabbalah, from its first blossoming, the form in which it first presented itself, through its many further developments and up to the present moment.

Collecting and publishing the manuscripts scattered across the globe would be as vital a part of this project as dating and reconstructing the Kabbalah in its origins and transformations.

Scholem wanted his research to deliver an answer to the question he posed when he began, and to which he returned again and again over the course of decades: 'Is there something of value in the Kabbalah or not?'

By 'Kabbalah' Scholem denotes Jewish mysticism with its esoteric literature since the twelfth century, whose genesis the young Scholem resolved to describe. It was a bold, near-impossible endeavour. In the half century that followed he investigated the sources of the Kabbalah and its major stages, in particular the Pseudepigraphic *Sefer Ha-Zohar* ('The Book of Lights') and the Lurianic Kabbalah from after the expulsion of the Jews from Spain in 1492. Scholem prefaced his most extensive book – on the 'false one', the mystical Messiah Sabbatai Zevi (1626–1676) – with a half-sentence from the late-nineteenth-century correspondence between Wilhelm Dilthey and Count Paul Yorck von Wartenburg:

> ... that paradox is a mark of the truth; that *communis opinio* [common opinion] has surely no place in the truth, being an elementary deposit of generalizing quasi-understanding, which is to the truth as the sulphur fumes are to the lightning bolt which leaves them behind.

There could be no pithier summary of the essential character of Scholem's research. The Turkish Jew Sabbatai Zevi worked by paradox: Zevi, who presented himself before the Jews of Smyrna (modern İzmir) as the Messiah, the son of David, who spoke the unspeakable name of God, who transgressed the Commandments, was amoral and impulsive and ultimately converted to Islam. His impact is a paradox as well, because in Scholem's eyes it is precisely Zevi's apostasy that marks the beginning of modern Jewish history.

By turning his back on it, Sabbatai Zevi secured Judaism and prepared it for the changed conditions of the modern era. Sabbateanism is the first revolution from the inside of Jewish consciousness. Scholem wrote:

> The mystical heresy led among certain sections of its devotees to consequences of a more or less nihilistic character, to a religious anarchy on mystical foundations, which, where it met with propitious external conditions, played a large role in the inner preparation of the Enlightenment and Reform in Judaism in the nineteenth century.

David Biale has called Scholem's work a 'counter-history'; the mainstream of the Jewish Enlightenment either ignored the wellsprings that Scholem later gathered together or allowed them to dry out entirely.

Scholem's listed profession contains within it a grain of irony. In October 1937 Scholem described to his publisher, Salman Schocken, how he became a 'Kabbalist'. He put the word in quotation marks, an indication of the distance inherent to his method for interpreting something of which one does not wholly approve. Scholem wrote:

> To show that myth and pantheism are "false" has no place in my work at all – it seemed far more important to me to note, as in the beginning a devout Jew had to me, that

nevertheless there was something in it. Such a higher order, be it ever so distorted, I sensed in the Kabbalah. It seemed to me that here, beyond the discernment of my generation, an empire of connections existed, which must also touch on our most human experiences. Granted that the key to understanding it seemed to be lost, judging by the dismal level of enlightenment Jewish scholars had offered on the subject. And yet here, in the first books of the Kabbalists, as I read them with fervent incomprehension, something flashed forth too astonishingly, a thinking which plainly – to use a Berlin expression – had not yet found its way home. […] My work lives, today as on my first day, in this paradox, in just such a hope of being addressed truthfully from the mountain, of that tiny, thoroughly inconspicuous displacement of history, which allows the truth to burst forth from the appearance of "evolution".

Scholem laid out fundamental considerations for his work at the start. In the 1930s he wrote 'Ten Unhistorical Aphorisms on Kabbalah', a key text for understanding his future work and his method. They consist in essence of ten variations on one paradox:

[The] Kabbalist claims there is a tradition of truth which it is possible to bequeath. An ironic claim, because the truth in question is anything but bequeathable. It can be recognised but not handed down and precisely that in it which can be handed down no longer contains it. Authentic tradition remains concealed; only a tradition in decline lands on an object and only as it declines can its greatness be seen.

The stance is ironic, to endure this paradox, but irony here is understood as a holding back from speaking about your own motivations, even the impulses of your own religiosity. Scholem writes of his hope that he will be addressed from the mountain, not of the fulfilment of this hope. That he is no atheist is the limit of what Scholem will betray to others.

In Scholem, a Kabbalist had made his way into Jerusalem, who, unlike the Kabbalists in Safed, did not understand these teachings as a way of life; who did not seek to achieve the *unio mystica* through practice, ways of speaking, music or erotically charged images, but rather by the methods of historical philology.

His entry in the directory runs:

(Family Name) Prof. Scholem
(First Name) Gershom
(Profession or Work) Kabbalist
(Workplace) University
(Street) Ramban
(Name of Homeowner) Prof. Scholem
(House No.) 51

Scholem was a book collector from early on, chiefly in his field of research, the Kabbalah, but with forays into literary antiquarian bookshops in Berlin or Munich, where he purchased first editions. His library includes the first edition of Lichtenberg's pseudonymously published satire of 1773, on the occasion of Lavater's attempt to convert Moses Mendelssohn: *Timorus. A Defence of Two Israelites, who, Swayed by the Vigour of the Lavaterian Arguments in Proof and of the Göttingenian*

Pork Sausages, Embraced the True Faith. Alongside that is a small bound copy of the same title from his father's library, which Scholem received from his older brother fifty years later: 'Gift from Reinhold on 15 March 1978. Sumptuous binding by Meink, master bookbinder of Berlin, inscribed by Alice Graman-Horodisch'. There is a handprinted edition of the *Letters on the Talmud* (1795) exchanged between Jean Paul and Emanuel Osmund, alongside the scarce edition of Jean Paul's collected works from 1826. And the first edition of Stefan George's *The Year of the Soul*, early printings of Scheerbart's novellas, some rare Kafka editions, Marcel Proust's *In Search of Lost Time*, works by Julien Green and Karl Kraus and autographed copies of works by Nelly Sachs (whom Scholem met in Stockholm), Max Frisch, Elias Canetti, Paul Celan and others.

By 1982 his library encompassed some 25,000 volumes. Today it contains over 35,000 and is expanding still. Scholem, who meticulously recorded his acquisitions and the books he was seeking, wrote in 1968 that he hoped at the end of his life to bequeath to the National Library of Israel approximately 2,000 Hasidic texts, 3,000 works of the Kabbalah, 500 to 600 books on Sabbateanism, 600 on Hasidism and 1,700 on Merkabah, Jewish magic and other subjects. And he added that he expected to achieve his aim by 1980. Gershom Scholem died in February 1982. Soon after, his books were taken from Rehavia into the National Library in neighbouring Givat Ram, where they were preserved as a separate collection in the 'Hadrei Gershom Scholem'. These rooms house the only private collection in the National Library. Today one sees many Orthodox Jews there studying Scholem's books: those whom he declared – whether soberly or passionately, sincerely or ironically – to be the object of his research have instead, it seems, joined the ranks of the researchers.

On the shelves we find Joseph Klausner's *From Jesus to Paul* and *Jesus of Nazareth* from the Jüdischen Verlag, Alfons Rosenberg's *The Soul's Journey* and a book on *Rebirth, Metempsychosis or Ascension through the Spheres* with a chapter on the idea of reincarnation in Kabbalist teaching. Scholem collected esoteric works as well, novels by Gustav Meyrink and works by Oskar Goldberg on alchemy and occultism. We may discover Ludwig Klages's *Stefan George*, published in 1902 by Georg Bondi in Berlin, or Gustav Karpeles's *History of Jewish Literature*, inscribed by hand – 'Gerhard Scholem. 2nd December 1911' – three days before his fourteenth birthday. There are works by Baudelaire and Fontane, a Wilhelm Busch album, Ernst Bloch's *The Spirit of Utopia* and *Sebastian Franck: A German Seeker* by Will-Erich Peuckert, published by Piper Verlag in Munich in 1943.

Betty Scholem made a significant contribution to the formation of her son's library. On 19 February 1929 she wrote to her son:

> Now we come to this Talmud. My dear child, I must solemnly refuse such a sea serpent. I can under no circumstances take on this burden! The Bible in question would have required four years at 25 marks, I would have been paying for it each year until it was complete, but then I could not have bought my way down this & that wish list alongside this, I'd have had to alternate instead. The Neumark & the contemporary Hermes make 25 marks

already! – But to get involved in this thing with 11 volumes, with this constant toing & froing, one volume is supposed to appear & I'm supposed to worry about it every hour of the day & then it still hasn't been published at all & I'm endlessly enquiring after it & your endless dilly-dallying! No, sir! This you cannot expect.

In fact, quite a number of these sea serpents did make their way from Berlin to Jerusalem.

In his diary Scholem meticulously recorded the 'addition of books since 5th XII 1933'; four years later he wrote a booklet, *Alu le-Shalom* – Scholem took the title from Jacob's words to his sons, 'Go in peace' – offering a list of his desiderata on Kabbalah and Jewish mysticism, from David F. Megerlin's *Hidden Testaments to the Truth of the Christian Religion, Drawn from Judaic Amulets and Phylacteries* (Frankfurt, 1756) via Michael Wormser's *The Life and Works of Rabbi Seckel Löb Wormser, Late of Michelstadt* (Offenbach, 1853) and Friedrich A. Tholuck's *De Ortu Cabbalae* (Hamburg, 1837) through to numerous titles in Hebrew. Over the years, in most cases, these too found their way to Scholem.

Inside the books, the dedications and notes, question and exclamation marks in Scholem's hand tell us a great deal about him and his connections. The *German Reader*, edited by Hugo von Hofmannsthal, in its second, enlarged edition, bears the dedication 'Gerhard and Escha Scholem's wedding gift from my Paris apartment / 8 September 1927 / Walter Benjamin'. The apartment foreshadows Benjamin's later place of exile, where he and Scholem would see each other for the last time. The book tells us of Benjamin's relationship to Hofmannsthal and indicates how strongly its Parisian sender felt linked to the circle of German culture. We find other dedications from Adorno and Elias Canetti, from German as well as Israeli writers and scholars.

'6 months earlier', 'brazen, but false', 'entirely invented' and 'unspeakable falsehood' writes Scholem in the margins of Hannah Arendt's essay on Walter Benjamin. His decisive, often furious annotations add much to the story of Scholem's dispute with the philosopher in New York: traces of a book's use that ripple out into the world.

Mother's Boy: Betty and Gershom Scholem

Betty Scholem visited her son Gershom in Jerusalem three times, at intervals of five years each time. She wrote on 6 January 1931:

> I come now to our voyage, & have great pleasure in inform-
> ing you that we yesterday booked our tickets with Cook's,
> after Erich performed the somewhat painful amputation
> of Egypt. Egypt takes 12–14 days & costs minimum 1,000
> Marks – he has neither the time nor the money. [...] I
> have written out our tour, as we finally fixed it yesterday,
> on the sheet enclosed. After that we'll meet in Jerusalem on
> Tuesday the 31st of March. The boat home (Haifa–Trieste)
> leaves always on a Wednesday, so he cannot take that on
> 01.04, we're reckoning on the 08.04 instead, and perhaps
> we'll wander a little longer in Syria with the time & come
> to Jerusalem a few days later, though on the other hand,
> the Seder takes place on 01.04 & Erich wants to experience
> that in Yerushalayim. Well, we'll see.

And the mother addressed a point vital to her travel planning:

Re: your belief that 2,500 M. will be very tight for me. We've reckoned on 2,000 for Erich, I'm staying 3–4 weeks longer, but won't I just have to get by? Mind you, my calculations this time, of necessity I'm afraid, make *no allowance* for your "appetites"!! You cannot be cadging off me or robbing me, nor can I renew your wardrobe for you, nor am I in a position to cough up for every bill that happens to present itself while I'm there, nor for the barbers, rounding up & a bonus for honesty, which constituted a sizable item in 1926 & properly amused Lene Cohn when we went through my little book. This time you have to make do! If anything, I expect you to be paying my debts!

The following week Gerhard answered from Jerusalem:

Darling Mother, don't let yourself be fooled! 2,500 M. is tight. You are not sufficiently taking into account that a tourist, even if his main purpose is to exchange gossip, remains nevertheless a tourist. Our home is very lovely, but you will surely sometimes want to go to a café or the cinema, the theatre, the cabaret. You will not be so indolent as to wish only to sit between 4 walls the whole time, on the grounds that it costs nothing there. You also surely will not suggest that we poor already too scrimping public officials can be leading such exalted lives. You will also want here and there on occasion to invite us along. You will want to see all the colourful oriental things and buy something for children and grandchildren. After you have seen the inside of the local buses you will in fact experience some mild anxiety and will at some point want to take a taxi. In short, no matter what, you will want to lead your life and you will have to lead your life and that costs something more than the life of a slightly exalted office worker.

The travel money was sufficient. The generous and pliable mother – who had long worked as a bookkeeper at the Scholem printworks and looked after their domestic accounts as well – did not broach the topic with her son again, at least on this occasion. For her trips to Palestine, Betty Scholem chose always the mild Jerusalem spring; on her last, in 1936, the seventy-year-old left the tribulations of National Socialist Germany behind her: Werner's arrest, the harassment by the authorities, the threats and lawlessness. All of which – save for during the short summer of the Olympic Games in Berlin in 1936 – grew dramatically worse on her return. Betty Scholem often thought back to her time in Jerusalem in happy anticipation, longingly and desperately – in her native Berlin no less than in distant, unfamiliar Sydney, which she reached, after atrocious hardships, 'naked as a jaybird' – as she wrote on 23 February 1939 to 'my dear child'.

The correspondence between mother and son could be the basis of a fascinating film: the journeys from Berlin to Jerusalem, but also the two cities, intercut over two decades. In Germany the political instability of the twenties, the world economic crisis reaching its apogee in 1929; in Palestine the years of construction and the Yishuv endangered by unrest; the fateful year 1933, Gershom's trips to Germany and Europe in 1932 and 1938, mother and son's last meeting on 28 March 1939 in Port Said. The letters hold up a mirror in which you see a vivid image of their times. Even if you strip out from Gerhard's letters a son's customary duty of care – to protect his mother and prettify his own life – they remain a lively and revealing historical document.

'Well! I hope you are not spinning your Kabbalistic thread for nothing & blasting in the quarry just for the kudos?' asked his mother of the just-emigrated Gerhard, who had found his first job at the National Library. In September 1924 she wrote to her son, who had been trying to encourage his mother:

> You talk of memoirs! That is harder to do than people think. The number of times I've considered it, whether I could make a start at writing the family history, and every time I realize it doesn't work. Or I'd have to restrict myself to basic data, without all the ironical framing or Bengali flourishes. There are some people I'd have to say that he's a larger-than-life creep & then maybe his offspring still know him & don't agree one bit and I'm left being the nasty one! And should I be chewing over the nonsense that so many other people have already cultivated and rehashed? Should anyone immortalize what, seen from a longer perspective, ought really to be called mere tittle-tattle? For example, the main things her contemporaries see of Borcharden are that she pilfers cigars and tells lies. And yet she is a person of infinite value, thoroughly capable and vigorous, clever, obliging, entirely kind-hearted and of inexhaustible good cheer. To *me* grandfather Scholem seems not merely black but pitch black – and yet perhaps he was white?! De

mortuis *nil*, nisi bene! And on top of that, your own secret compartment you absolutely cannot open. "Oh!" I hear a distant grandchild cry, "thaaaat was how the old lady was wallpapered on the inside?!"

'The Jerusalem into which I arrived was as if ordained for me by heaven or at least it was like it was made for me. I felt at home there,' Scholem remembered. In his autobiography he described the awakening in the 1920s, the development of the country, the solidarity among the numerically small Yishuv. Scholem rejected a job as a maths teacher and took up Shmuel Hugo Bergmann's offer to work in the National Library from half seven in the morning to two o'clock in the afternoon. In the morning he would be surrounded by books which would have interested him anyway; in the afternoon he had time left to do his own writing. Thus the most fascinating library in book-rich Rehavia came into being.

Guest Arabs: Brit Shalom

Escha Scholem wrote on 17 April 1932 to her husband Gerhard in Rome:

> The club has met again since then, with some guest Arabs from outside Jerusalem in fact, who were thoroughly nice. But then something odd happened again. Karmi was summoned in front of the party's disciplinary tribunal, to give the details of what had supposedly been a private meeting. Whether he's already attended and what came out of it, I haven't been able to find out.

The club in question is Brit Shalom (literally, 'Covenant of Peace') and that casual reference to 'guest Arabs' brings centre stage what was already by then a long-running conflict and the attempts to understand and defuse it. Founded in 1925 by Arthur Ruppin, Brit Shalom was an association of mostly German-Jewish immigrants, including Gershom Scholem, Ernst Simon, Shmuel Hugo Bergmann, Hans Kohn and Robert Weltsch from Prague, with the aim of establishing in Palestine a bi-national polity of Jews and Arabs. Brit Shalom's enrolled membership numbered sixty, the majority in Jerusalem, with around seventy-five friends, and it had support both inside and outside the country, from the likes of Martin Buber and Albert Einstein.

There had been tensions between the two peoples since the early 1920s, leading to bloody clashes in August 1929 in which 130 Jews and 116 Arabs were killed. Brit Shalom understood the attacks by the Arabs differently from the official Zionist organisations in Palestine: not as staged riots but as a nationalist uprising directed against Jewish settlement of the country. Its members clashed profoundly over whether the 'Covenant of Peace' ought to become directly involved in politics or merely submit suggestions to the Zionist organisations in Palestine, in order to smooth over the clashes if not to remedy them. Years before Israel's independence, the question was how such a state should be founded and constituted, as a confederation within a state on the Habsburg model, allowing peoples their national and cultural autonomy in a supranational frame. Michael Brenner has shown how most of the representatives of this influential group repudiated the traditional model of the nation state, preferring instead a concept – 'homeland'

– which left ample leeway for elaboration. Position papers were composed, petitions lodged, articles published, conventions held. Its members met up mostly in Rehavia, with the addition of some 'guest Arabs' from time to time. That casual phrase of Escha Scholem's names Brit Shalom's blind spot. The Jewish inhabitants kept largely to themselves. Brit Shalom finally dissolved itself in 1933; the disturbances of 1929 and strengthening nationalism on both sides hastened its dissolution.

No German-language writer has captured the atmosphere of Jerusalem in that fateful year of unrest more densely than Arnold Zweig in his novel *De Vriendt Goes Home*. Published in 1932, it remained on open sale for only one winter and even later, after the war, had as difficult a reception in the divided Germany as it did in Israel. Zweig, who would later emigrate to Palestine, had visited the territory earlier in 1932 and revived his plan of some years before to compose a novella based on a historical murder: that of the Dutch writer and jurist Israël de Haan. De Haan was born into an Orthodox Jewish family in Amsterdam in 1881 and emigrated to Jerusalem in 1918. Quite soon, however, he turned his back on Zionism, becoming spokesman for an association of Orthodox Jews and speaker of the Ashkenazi Council, two groups striving from early on to achieve an accommodation between Jews and Arabs. Gershom and Escha Scholem met de Haan at the house of the doctor Moshe Wallach; as soon as he learned of the couple's Zionist views he unleashed fire and brimstone on their heads and prophesied them a bad end. A year later, on a summer evening in 1924, de Haan was shot dead on a public street in Jerusalem. At first people wondered if the killing had been an act of vengeance by the Arab family of de Haan's young lover Saud, until it became apparent that he had been killed by radical Zionists.

Zweig shifted this historical killing to the year 1929 with all its political tensions, and set the inner turmoil of 'de Vriendt', as he called de Haan, against the outward scenery of the ever-expanding holy city:

> Outside in Rehavia the new villa district and the large block intended to house the Jewish self-government, the Zionist People's Fund [also known as the Jewish National Fund], were rising up. For the moment, they were still sitting here in the business district, close to the Central Post Office, while the Arab executive had settled in the area around Damascus Gate.

The boundaries that divide Jerusalem to this day were already visible in 1929.

Utopian Rehavia: Walter Benjamin

In his first autobiographical book, *Walter Benjamin: The Story of a Friendship*, two years before his memoirs were published, Scholem describes how he wanted to bring his friend to Jerusalem. In the summer of 1927 Scholem had brought together Walter Benjamin and Judah Leon Magnes, the then Chancellor (and later President) of the Hebrew University, which was supposed to be getting a humanities faculty. What a fascinating, sparks-flying conversation there must have been between the three men! Benjamin talked about his intent to approach the great texts of Jewish literature through the medium of Hebrew, not as a philologist but as a metaphysician. Benjamin's self-description as a metaphysician, which seems almost fantastical today, fell on sympathetic ears.

Magnes, an American rabbi, had studied in Heidelberg. He was open-minded, politically on the far left and had a mastery of German. He asked the candidate how he imagined preparing for such a task:

> Benjamin said that, provided he had the financial wherewithal to do it, he would ideally come to Jerusalem for a year, where he could devote himself exclusively to studying the language and discover whether he had the capability not only to find his way into the sources, but also to express himself adequately as an academic teacher in Hebrew.

Magnes promised to think the matter over and take expert advice.

On 30 January 1928 Benjamin wrote to Scholem:

> This is perhaps the last time I will have the chance to turn my attention to Hebrew and all that is for us associated with that. It is also a thoroughly opportune time. For one thing, it is in accord with my inner readiness. If I can somehow conclude the work upon which I am currently, carefully, tentatively engaged – this very curious and precarious experiment *Parisian Arcades: A Dialectical Féerie* (I have never written anything at such a risk of failure) – then one cycle of work, the *One-Way Street* cycle, will be

complete, in the same way that my tragedy book brought my studies of German literature to an end.

Benjamin went on to request a stipend of '300 Marks per month for the duration of my accelerated study' of Hebrew. In March Benjamin eagerly took up Scholem's suggestion that he could teach German and French literature in Jerusalem, and in May was still writing to Scholem:

> I have put an autumn visit to Palestine firmly into my year planner. I'm hoping to have clarity from Magnes before-hand on the financial basis of my period of study. My heartfelt thanks to you both for your invitation. I would naturally be delighted to stay with you for a few weeks, if you can arrange it.

Gershom and Escha Scholem – she was an outstanding Hebrew teacher – were sceptical about what the going monthly rate was in Berlin; in Jerusalem the same amount would have allowed Benjamin to study the language without any other earnings. Magnes, however, quite unexpectedly wired the entire figure for the proposed stipend to Benjamin. Benjamin then cancelled his trip for the autumn and held out the prospect of his coming in early 1929. But this too he cancelled, partly for external reasons, but far more for internal ones. This all happened at the same time as a 'Russian friend' came to Benjamin, Asja Lacis, with whom he had fallen in love and who would later boast that she 'prevented' his trip. Whether or not that is so – and there's significant evidence to suggest it was – Benjamin never went to Jerusalem. In the summer of 1929 he took a few hours of Hebrew tuition with the private scholar Dr Max Mayer in Berlin, but after going travelling he never resumed his lessons.

Almost fifty years later Scholem recalled this 'failed project' and its 'utopian aspect'. At the time Benjamin had seemed to imagine that the theological categories of Judaism were a vanishing point for his thinking. Benjamin was to a significant degree deceiving himself, especially after the failure of his academic career, over his own bond to the world of Europe. On top of which, there is something that Scholem did not mention, because he was so much part of that world: the date. In 1927 and 1928 it was still mandatory to have acquired the language of the country to secure a teaching position at the Hebrew University. In later years, especially with the immigration after the events of 1933, this tended to be overlooked. If Walter Benjamin had come to Jerusalem at the end of the 1920s to learn Hebrew for some months, it would have opened up the possibility of emigration later, a possibility denied him after 1933 following the failure of his project four years previously.

When Scholem, working with Theodor W. Adorno, published Benjamin's letters in the mid-1960s, leftist critics in particular criticised him for having wanted to 'persuade' Benjamin to come to Palestine and for pitting the Jewish-theological dimension of his work against his Marxist-materialist side. Scholem pointed out in response, surely rightly, that no one could have persuaded a personality as complex as Benjamin, even had he wanted to.

Yet for a moment one imagines it: that Benjamin had set out on his journey and later had emigrated to Palestine. Walter

Benjamin in Rehavia, a long way from Berlin or Paris, but in the company of Scholem, Bergmann, Guttmann, later of Martin Buber, Werner Kraft, Else Lasker-Schüler and many others. What exchanges might have taken place? What would have been the possibilities and limits? What might have been changed? Rehavia was always the place of utopia for those who did not manage to get there. In 1933 Walter Benjamin emigrated to Paris. In the summer of 1940, on the run from the Nazis, he took his own life on the French–Spanish border. Scholem had collected and preserved his friend's writings from the early days. As a result, one of the most important collections of Benjamin's papers lies today in the National Library in Jerusalem and in Berlin.

Concubine: A Club in Jerusalem

Un-imaginary Portraits was the name Shmuel Sambursky gave to the poems he accumulated over the years and brought out in a slim volume in 1960. Sambursky, born in 1900 into a Jewish-Russian family in Königsberg, came to Jerusalem in 1924 and took on the teaching position which his friend Gerhard had rejected in favour of the library. In 1928 the two became colleagues at the newly opened Hebrew University. Sambursky, a disarming and curious scholar of both the sciences and the humanities taught physics and the history of science. I met him and his wife Miriam in 1986, by which time the pair had lived at 28 Ben Maimon Boulevard for half a century. Over the years Sambursky had become the chronicler of a unique circle in Rehavia, a group of scholars who had met together in their homes from the 1930s onwards. The group called itself

'Pilegesh', the biblical word for a concubine, formed from the first letter of each of their names (originally 'Pil', Hebrew for 'elephant', from the Egyptologist Hans Polotsky, the philosopher Hans Jonas, the classical philologist Hans Lewy, and Scholem). The members were mostly bachelors – hence the self-ironising, innuendo-laden name for their gatherings – and met on Shabbat afternoons to discuss problems in their various subjects, as well as the questions of the day, over coffee and cake.

Though the format of their meetings has been passed down to us, the contents have sadly not. 'I have to say, that the intellectual climate in Jerusalem in those years was magnificent,' recalled Hans Jonas in an interview with Rachel Salamander:

We were all people in the prime of our lives and our intellectual development. Each one of us in his own way was interesting and we were all different. [...] In short, everybody had something to say and we said it with exceptional thoroughness. There was never a boring moment or a shortage of themes, quite apart from the events of the day, which we commented on in our conversations. And it was all in German! Here we were, we had found each other in Jerusalem, the holy city, in that Palestine with its Jewish settlements destined by Zionism for a renewal of the life of the Jewish people. George Lichtheim and I excepted, all of us worked at the Hebrew University and – albeit to varying degrees – were excellent Hebraists, Scholem and Sambursky especially. And yet in our private conversations we clung to German – not from any connection with Germanness, but simply because it was for us the natural language, in which we were best able to express ourselves.

The copy of his parodic and self-mocking poems that Shmuel Sambursky gave me in January 1990 happens to contain the draft of a letter from 1970, in which he introduced the protagonists of Pilegesh: George Lichtheim, the youngest member in Pilegesh, in 'Portrait of a Thirty-Year-Old'; the botanist Ephraim Hareuveni in 'The Nudnik' (Yiddish for 'pain in the neck'); the endocrinologist Hermann Zondek in 'Apotheosis of the Hormones'; and Gershom Scholem in 'Scholem's Secret', a piece of light raillery on Scholem's interest in mysticism and the esoteric, addiction to gambling and penchant for marzipan:

Our Scholem keeps a demon horde
Who lodge *chez lui*, with bed and board.
They owe him thanks on lavish scale
As every day he tells their tale.
He builds their fame without a let-up:
It really is a pleasant set-up.
Though there's no way that they can meet
His rampant spend on all things sweet,
His impish chums instead produce
In every field the coming news,
On marriage, divorce, on peace and war,
And whate'er else we men endure.
Info acquired, he bets his dough –
He knows that none can save his foe.
Thus murky beings spare him bother,

And mental angst and costs brackets other,
And tongue on tooth our Scholem can
Already taste sweet marzipan.

The poem is dated 5 December 1939, Scholem's forty-second birthday, evidently the date Sambursky presented it to his friend.

The inhabitants of Rehavia lived in separate, more-or-less closed circles. They knew each other, gave reciprocal invitations, kept themselves pretty much to themselves – as a note, written on 21 November 1936 by Erich Brauer, a childhood friend of Scholem from his Berlin days, shows almost in passing:

> On Shabbat I go to eat and when you go for a walk like that around Rehavia, even me who doesn't really know many people, I'm being stopped and embraced by all sorts. I bump into the Goiteins and then the Tichos. Frau Ticho is playing with me a bit. I act like I don't notice and she insists on inviting me over for Wednesday, to look at her stuff.

Shlomo Dov Goitein was a well-known Arabist in Rehavia. Anna Ticho was a painter. Her husband, Dr Albert Ticho, set up Jerusalem's first eye hospital, famous for its successes in treating eye conditions caused by the climate in Palestine. Today the Ticho House is a museum complete with café, close to Jaffa Street.

Rehavia was home to professors, clerical staff and students of the Hebrew University, which at the time of its inauguration in 1925 was fundamentally influenced by German-Jewish scholars. Gershom and Escha Scholem, Shmuel Hugo Bergmann, Shmuel Sambursky, Joseph Klausner, Hayim Nahman Bialik and many others were present at the ceremony on 1 April on Mount Scopus, as was the architect Lotte Cohn:

We had climbed upwards, in the company of a mass migration of Jews; perhaps it wasn't really that many people, but it wasn't the number that counted, it was the feeling: intellectual Jewry was climbing the mountain. The mountain – and, as it seemed to us, the world – had come to life in a unique, unanimous desire to pay tribute and respect to the mind and to scholarship. A Jewish university was being consecrated. There they stand, against the backdrop of this magnificent landscape, these men, the bearers of the idea, and those who had helped to make it a reality. Weizmann in the violet robes appropriate to his academic rank. There one sees the fine head of Dr. Magnes, who will be the first Dean of the university. Rav Kook, the country's Chief Rabbi. And now Lord Balfour steps up onto the platform, archetype of the "British nobility", tall and exceptionally handsome. He too is in the garb of his rank: his robes are scarlet. The sun is setting, the last rays fall on his face as he addresses the gathering. There they stand, these men, representatives of thought in Eretz Israel, one feels the emotion in their words. A promise is being made: that this University should be a witness to the world for Judaism and for Jewish thought. What a moment in our intellectual history… and what an image to symbolize it.

An impassioned, resolute, yet in reality humble beginning. Already at the first Zionist Congress of 1897 in Basel participants had called for a distinct Jewish educational institution. Now Baron Rothschild was supporting the project, on the condition that the result should be not an ordinary university but rather a research institute. The University, founded in 1918, received no money from the government in Palestine and was instead dependent on private donations. In 1925 it consisted of a small institute for Jewish studies, at which Scholem worked, which nonetheless experienced such a rush of people that it could enroll "auditors" alongside the actual students. A humanities faculty was established in 1928; courses of study in the natural sciences began in 1931. The first chair in Jewish Philosophy was awarded in 1934 to Julius Guttmann, born in Hildesheim and grown up in Breslau, whose *The Philosophy of Judaism*, published 1933, achieved worldwide acclaim.

On 15 November 1938, seventeen-year-old Walter Laqueur made it to Jerusalem in an armoured bus: the 'Revolts', as they were called, of the Arab population were in full swing. Ten days earlier the young Laqueur had still been in Nazi Germany. His train from Breslau to Trieste, where he would embark for Palestine, had crossed the border just as the pogrom in Germany began. In the winter of 1938, Laqueur enrolled at the Hebrew University, which had then around 800 students. His subject, modern history, was led by Richard Koebner, who lived at 34 Abarbanel Street, three houses along from Gershom Scholem. Between the two lived Richard Kauffmann, in the heart of the neighbourhood he had built. Three long and entirely distinct life paths crossing in one short street.

Richard Koebner, born in Breslau in 1885, did not arrive in

Palestine until he was almost fifty, after the Nazi authorities had removed him from his position in 1933. As a university lecturer he had specialised in medieval history, German urban history and rural forms of settlement. One of his pupils records the difficulties Koebner experienced in giving his lectures in Hebrew and in translating into this new language terms which had preoccupied him throughout his career, such as 'Landfrieden' (a legal declaration in the Holy Roman Empire, outlawing violence to resolve disputes) and 'Zaudengericht' (a Silesian term for a court concerned with the law of property and inheritance). He was no less at home in more recent periods of history, his new subject areas, but here too were profound problems of translation: how to render 'revolution' and 'reform', 'rural depopulation' and 'reparation negotiations' into Hebrew? Or the idea of 'colonies', which the Zionists used to describe their first settlements? The Hebrew equivalent – 'moshava' – means 'settlement' as well as 'colony'. In spite of all these difficulties Koebner trained generations of history teachers in Palestine and Israel. Today the Center for German History at the Hebrew University is named for him. In 1953 he emigrated and lived thereafter in London until his death in 1958.

The Sorcerer's Apprentice: George Lichtheim

George Lichtheim called Scholem his 'master sorcerer'. The sorcerer's apprentice, son of the Zionist politician and theorist Richard Lichtheim, was the youngest member of Pilegesh – he was in his mid-twenties – and a close friend of Scholem. The spirits they summoned live on in their notably vociferous and fiery correspondence. On one occasion Lichtheim writes to his friend that he would like to box Scholem's ears for his 'boorishness'. As a historian of ideas Lichtheim had a deep knowledge of the history of Marxism and socialism, of critical theory and of Moses Hess – themes and figures that barely made an appearance in Scholem's work, but which he pursued in their correspondence. Though the difference in their ages might have suggested it, there was nothing of the 'teacher-pupil' in Scholem and Lichtheim's relationship; the teacher had too much to learn from the pupil and the pupil had too little desire to learn from the teacher. Lichtheim had never really had a teacher – no more than Scholem had, albeit in another sense. In the late 1930s Lichtheim, whose mastery of English was on a level with his German, worked with Scholem to devise a series of lectures on the fundamentals of Jewish mysticism. From 1946 Lichtheim lived in London and wrote a succession of books on Marxism, the concept of ideology and Europe and America, as well as superb essays on Adorno, Lukács and Benjamin. In a birthday letter on 28 November 1966, he wrote to Scholem from London:

> I must also admit that as I often recall my years in Jerusalem I from time to time ask myself whether it was not a mistake to have left. It is undeniable that in your country one at least does not have that feeling of being 'in a foreign land', which is unavoidable here. In the end I too simply departed, because only here could I do my real work: there we are back on the same theme. – As ever, reading Benjamin's letters in these circumstances has strengthened my soul. Perhaps it is because the Weimar period is on the rise

again – at any rate one feels personally affected on almost every page. In this spirit, Your Lichtheim.

He twice wrote letters of farewell to the master sorcerer in Jerusalem. On the first occasion his suicide attempt failed. On 22 April 1973 in London, George Lichtheim took his own life.

When Lichtheim quit Jerusalem in 1945, Pilegesh had already disbanded. Hans Jonas had travelled into Germany with British troops and returned to Israel during the War of Independence, before finally emigrating to Canada in 1949.

The sabbaths trickled past them like a stream
That ever thinner flows and then no more.
The later years were but a wan reflection
Of that first time, which lies so long before

That they've romanticized it on the sly:
Those dazzling duels and scholarly disputes
Were not so common and always unforeseen.
They sat as often engaged in being mute,

For stretches which never left them dry,
When they were fruitful, shrewd, refined.
And in that ring of silence and of words
One unrelenting thing swept forward: time.

Thus Shmuel Sambursky turned his memory of Pilegesh's end into a poem, entitled 'The Club'.

Professor Unworldly: Escha and Gershom Scholem

Two works of world literature deal with Rehavia and both came into being on its periphery, their authors looking at that neighbourhood from the outside: Amos Oz from neighbouring Kerem Avraham and S.Y. Agnon from Talpiot, at most an hour's walk from Rehavia. One of the sad, ironically drawn heroes of Agnon's novel *Shira* is Ernst Weltfremd (German for 'Unworldly'), a friend of Manfred Herbst, the central character of the novel, who has taken up a chair in Jewish-Hellenistic literature at the Hebrew University. Agnon's heroes remain unhappy because none of them find fulfilment: Manfred Herbst doesn't in his erotic encounter with Shira, the nurse he meets while taking his wife Henriette to the hospital for the delivery of their third child, and his academic career as a Byzantinist isn't successful either. Fulfilment is denied to Alfred Neu as much as it is to his niece Lisbet, Julian, Taglicht, Hemdat and Herbst's two daughters, Zahara and Tamara. Agnon portrays them all as lost in their new world, scraping a living, struggling to learn Hebrew or get a job that suits them, fearing for their relatives who have stayed behind in Germany. Agnon resisted the idea that his work should be read as a *roman à clef* – because that's the most natural way of reading it.

Several lightly defamiliarised traits of Scholem are incorporated in Ernst Weltfremd: He is 'Professor Gamur', Professor 'Done and Dusted', a full professor and an expert in his field who is alienated from people and childless.

Agnon knew Scholem from his time in Germany. Scholem's marriage to Escha Burchardt, we may suppose, also seemed 'unworldly' to Agnon. The correspondence of the husband-and-wife-to-be has recently become available, from the time of their first encounter in Munich during their student days of lectures, plans and mutual friends. Burchardt travelled to Jerusalem some time before Scholem and lived and worked in the house of Shmuel Hugo Bergmann. Reading her early letters from Jerusalem one becomes aware that Scholem's bride was already in 1922 and 1923 conducting an affair with the then married Bergmann, which did not preclude a tenderness and solicitude for her distant bridegroom. In 1923 she finally married Gerhard and in 1932 the two couples, Bergmann and Scholem, bought adjoining houses on Ramban Street. After nine years in Palestine, Scholem travelled to Europe for six months. In April 1932 his wife wrote to him in Rome:

> Day before yesterday we celebrated the Passover Seder very beautifully at Chamsin's. 5 minutes before the ritual I hastily invited Fräulein Freud, whom Hugo had spotted in her lit window as he walked past. She was happy to accept and afterwards we walked through a warm and song-filled Jerusalem at night dressed for high summer.

In 1936 Gershom Scholem married Fräulein Fania Freud and Escha married Hugo Bergmann. In the year of their divorce Escha wrote to Gerhard, 'It is for me as if you had died.' But in later years the friendship between the two of them revived.

Rediscovery: Werner Kraft

For over sixty years the address – 31 Alfasi Street – remained the same. For over sixty years the arrangement of the house, the furnishings, the division of the living room, dining room and workspace (which is part of the living room) and the ordering of the books remained the same. For six decades the inhabitants read literature predominantly in German, sometimes in French, and the newspaper in English in an orderly daily routine of fixed mealtimes, the hour's sleep in the afternoon, coffee and cake with recurring guests and new ones as well, the walk to the post office, the garden behind the house. This is the home of Werner Kraft, who learned so little Hebrew that he was later forced to communicate with his grandchildren in English; his son and daughter had learned German, whereas his wife Erna spoke Hebrew effortlessly.

I was born in Brunswick on 4.5.1896 and grew up in Hanover. I graduated from secondary school there in 1914. I was a soldier during the War and after the War studied German, French and philosophy in Freiburg and Hamburg. In 1925 I completed my doctorate under Professor Franz Schultz in Frankfurt a.M. with a thesis on 'Pope Joan in German Literature: Study of a Historical Motif'. In 1926 I took the higher civil service grade examination in academic librarianship in Leipzig and from 1927 was senior librarian at the State Library (formerly the Royal Library) of Lower Saxony in Hanover. In 1933 I lost my position at this library on account of the Law for the Purification of the Professional Civil Service and left Germany with my wife and two children. Since 1934 I have lived in Jerusalem, where most of the works detailed in my list of publications came into being, sometimes under very difficult external circumstances. In recent years I have received a pension from my former office in Hanover and have dedicated myself entirely to my work as a writer. Since the founding of the state of Israel I have had Israeli citizenship.

In such laconic and matter-of-fact terms Werner Kraft presented himself in 1958 to the German Research Foundation, which intended to support a monograph of his. He attached his list of publications and appended this paragraph to his curriculum vitae:

The determining experience of my youth was the great German poetry of Goethe and Hölderlin. Among the newer German poets, Rudolf Borchardt has decisively influenced me and he it was who gave direction to my intellectual life.

Kraft's doctoral supervisor, Franz Schultz, was the same professor who in the 1920s rejected Walter Benjamin's book on German tragic drama as his habilitation thesis (habilitation is a post-doctoral qualification allowing you to teach in a university) on the contemptible but telling basis that you could not grant lecturer status to 'Geist' (that is, 'spirit' or 'mind'). His closeness to and distance from Benjamin shaped Kraft's life.

Kraft's book finally appeared in 1961, published by Claassen Verlag in Hamburg: *Rudolf Borchardt: World of Poetry and History*. Its author was as unfamiliar to the German public as the work of Borchardt, with which Kraft was concerned. Kraft had published his poems in German in Jerusalem: *Words from the Void* in 1937, *Poems I* a year later and *Poems II* in 1946.

His first book in Germany after the Second World War – following selections of poems by Else Lasker-Schüler (1951) and Karl Kraus (1952) – appeared from Verlag Lambert Schneider in Heidelberg as a publication of the German Academy for Language and Literature. Its title was programmatic of Kraft's entire life's work: *Rediscovery*. Most of the selected authors are from the nineteenth century – Kleist, Immermann, Grillparzer, Friedrich Schlegel – while others reach back into the eighteenth – Goethe, Jean Paul, Novalis, Schmidt von Lübeck. One has to remember the extent to which anthologies after the Second World War were seeking at first simply to acquaint people with authors and their works, a process begun by Richard Drews and Alfred Kantorowicz's 1947 anthology *Banned and Burned: Twelve Years of Suppressed German Literature*.

Kraft's early poetry selections appeared in the series *Lost and Forgotten*. But Karl Kraus and Else Lasker-Schüler are in fact missing from Kraft's anthology. What did he want to rediscover and to allow his readers to discover? As Ernst-Peter Wieckenberg has pointed out, there are only three Jewish authors represented within it – Börne, Heine and Landauer – and none of the non-Jewish authors driven from Germany from 1933 onwards. Instead we have a collection of the unusual and forgotten, those who found themselves outside the spotlight of contemporary attention, a gathering of the modest, standing somewhat to one side of the grand boulevard of literary history.

The senior librarian from Hanover understood himself

first and foremost as an anthologist and editor, who wanted others to share in his discoveries, most of them written in short forms, as in Nestroy's aphorism: 'Only do not hasten to fulfil the will of the Evil One, before the old God can send an angel.' Christian Wagner was another he rediscovered for the German people. On 31 August 1935 he noted in his Jerusalem diary: 'Christian Wagner as lyric poet of the Third Reich! What a time!' In that month Nazi Germany celebrated the hundredth birthday of the poet, 'who died at a great age in 1918', as Kraft remarks in the foreword to his anthology. He belongs to the nineteenth century. And he goes on to say:

> The inclusion of German lyric poetry after 1900 would have brought *others* centre stage, alongside the well-known poets – and even those would be differently selected. The time for that has not yet come. For now, the image of the German lyric up to 1900 functions as our present, because the actual present is not yet far enough away for it to be allowed to be a distinct self. Whoever experiences the present as past, makes a mistake; the solution is to experience the past as the future.

This apologia for the nineteenth century is surprising at a moment when the twentieth century was already at least half over. What future in the past is Kraft talking about? Few poets show us more clearly than Wagner, who combines piety with the experience of nature, morality with freedom, mysticism with a daylight-clear consciousness, as in his short poem 'Do you have', which Kraft includes in his anthology as part of a comparatively large selection from the poet from Warmbronn:

In your armoury, eternal one, do you have
A hammer still and not a wedge
For me, this earth-surplus,
Not blessed and yet blessed?

In four lines, 'question-singing, answer-speaking', the aporias of human existence rhyme and form a word that will much appeal to Kraft: 'earth-surplus' ('Erdüberzähligen').

'In him the mystical is nothing more than the victorious faculty of perception of a liberated, thoroughly reasonable man,' said Peter Handke of Wagner and the 'frequent moments of happiness in his language'.

Reason and order, the service and submission of an anthologist, the objectivity and restraint of an editor, are all at work in Kraft, virtues which allow others to stand out – Karl Kraus or Rudolf Borchardt, the lyrics of the century before last – with no historical-philosophical theses, no theories, no daring images or metaphors. With Kraft we get only presenting, highlighting, rediscovering.

Kraft's life as an anthologist made his existence profoundly solitary. He did not belong with the scholars at the Hebrew University nor to Pilegesh. For his first two decades in Jerusalem he was cut off from any possibility of effect in Germany, France or England and, for reasons of language, from operating in Israel.

In his first years in Jerusalem he worked as librarian at the Centre de Culture Française. The beginning of the Second World War brought his pension payments from Nazi Germany to an end. For his family of four it was the beginning of years of adversity and deprivation, with half their home rented out in order to secure their meagre subsistence.

In the 1930s and 1940s Kraft became the literary ambassador of another Germany, ambassador for the Weimar Republic in Jerusalem. He took note of everything published after the rupture of 1933 but would not include it in his work. It gives his books, as well as his methodology, an aspect of conservation. German literature appears like a mosquito suspended flying in amber, polished to be recognisable, in a living past and yet in the present motionless.

In the 1950s, by his own efforts, Kraft found German readers, readers who would have been quite unthinkable in the years before. They were not many, but they were unusually loyal and engaged. Here too a rediscovery.

Gershom Scholem describes how, at the beginning of their friendship, having been brought together by Walter Benjamin during the years of the First World War, he worried that his new friend threatened to despair at the direction of his times. This trait Kraft retained for a long while; it seems that it was only in old age that he yielded to mirth, the kind of mirth of which Hegel says it is a joy that knows about grief.

'Night' is an early poem:

The sky entire blooms lilac
With the moon.
We must invent a new world.
This one weeps.

On 4 September 1934 Kraft, recently arrived in Jerusalem, wrote in his diary: 'The world is identical: whether in Hanover, Paris or Jerusalem – no difference for he who must live and die!' Almost terrified, the new immigrant noted in Rehavia:

'German Jews, under the splendid starry sky of Jerusalem, singing Lorelei – repulsive impression!' And a few weeks later, on 24 October, he wrote: 'Evening twilight. To express this or that thought in some half-way adequate form is still all I have left. – Everyone walks as if stooped. Not me actually. And yet I am sadder than everyone. Because I want more.'

In calling the fundamental nature of Kraft's literary-historical work 'conservation', one must not fall into the trap of thinking him conservative. He took a lively interest in Israeli politics and ended his anthology *Rediscovery* with Karl Kraus's famous poem on his falling silent in 1933: 'The word passed away as that world awoke.'

Kraft's verdicts on contemporary authors came out harshly:

Enzensberger is an abomination. Krolow is a washout who is slowly becoming representative. Celan is gifted but –? Bachmann, I'm not sure. But in the poems of Walter Helmut Fritz (Claassen) there's something beautiful, for example in the poem "In England", especially the last stanza! Erich Fried, a very nice man in London: something could come from him. Greve: some strong poems. Today I've spoken "on tape" (15 minutes) about E.L. Schüler. It will be broadcast from Stuttgart (Church Radio) at some point. – Benn, like E. Jünger, is non-existent to me.

From the Parnassus of nineteenth-century literature, Kraft's verdicts seem apodictic – and for that very reason, precarious. He never forgave his near contemporary Ernst Jünger for his involvement in the Second World War – nor Gottfried Benn. Only Bertolt Brecht, whom Kraft had met back in

1928 in Berlin and then met there again in 1954, found some favour in his eyes. Yet what a grotesque misjudgement of the significance of Benn's work in post-war German literature! Kraft passed judgement on Huchel, who feuded with Kraft's friend Wilhelm Lehmann, and one of his poems: 'nothing but jarring reverberations of Celan in its propagation of his ruined "Death Fugue" ["Todesfuge"]'. And a few weeks later:

> *For me* even the famous "Death Fugue" touches on kitsch. I am not made the right way to be able to consider this all too gifted poem beautiful. "Death is a master from Germany", for all its sad weight of truth, has a damnably aesthetic ring to it, before which I seal up my eyes and I told the poet so, to his astonishment.

In Kraft's correspondence with Lehmann the resentments proliferate while the two remain silent, at any rate in their letters, over what will have weighed heavily upon them: Wilhelm Lehmann's life in Nazi Germany, his joining the Nazi Party, even if only on life-saving, tactical grounds, and the murder of Europe's Jews. In all the eloquence of the two friends, in all the riches of their correspondence, the past that lay closest behind them is barely mentioned between Eckernförde and Jerusalem. It seems as if Kraft later revised his verdict on Celan, just as he from time to time interrupted himself with an admonishment for being unjust.

In her work on the literary canon of exiled German-Jewish authors, Caroline Jessen shows how difficult it was for Kraft to publish in Germany, even after 1945, and to hold his ground as a lyric poet as well. Added to which, editorial departments expected, with some justice, that an author from Israel might write something about Israel: articles on the history or politics of the country or modern Hebrew literature. These Kraft neither would nor could provide. In December 1971, Hans Paeschke, editor of the cultural journal *Merkur*, wrote to his occasional author in Jerusalem: 'Nowadays authors in the magazine should be in a conversation with the future, not the past'. And in response to Kraft's proud assertion that he would win through 'by tortoise steps', Paeschke responded on New Year's Eve 1971: 'That is why I am asking you over and over for your word on Israel. And if you could combine it with a discussion, perhaps on the memoirs of Nahum Goldmann? Why do you remain so tenaciously silent on this question?'

Werner Kraft remained so tenaciously silent on it because he did not understand himself as an Israeli author, nor even a Jewish one. 'My assimilation into German culture is so unproblematic that I feel myself free and happy as a Jew, without the slightest mental burden, unlike Borchardt, unlike Kraus even,' Kraft wrote in his diary in January 1935. The literature of the nineteenth century was his portable homeland, again and again he recalled the authors forgotten by the wayside, the luminosity of lyric images, of moral insights and aphorisms. Once he had arrived in his definitive exile, the entire world, be it Hanover, Paris or Jerusalem, seemed to him, in comparison with these, identical. The image remains unchanged over decades: Kraft lived as if suspended in amber, with living impulses, motifs, movements from earlier times, which he presented, fixed, to a furiously changing world. Some poems excepted, the essence of his work would not have turned out differently had Kraft emigrated to Gothenburg or to London. As for perhaps no other person, his exile was the words he carried with him. Kraft's daughter Alisa remembers:

> Throughout my childhood and later as well, it was my father who put me to bed. He bathed me in the evening, told me a story and put me to bed. So I grew up with the best German literature could offer me. Grimms' fairy tales, Andersen [sic], Hauff, Schwab's *Classical Antiquity*, German mythology and, as I grew older, Schiller, Goethe, Hauptmann, Wedekind and Brecht. He read aloud to me his whole life long in fact, works he loved and believed I would enjoy too. I believe that as a result my German is relatively good and I have some knowledge of German literature.

Kraft made notes not only on the events of the day and his impressions of his reading; he also paid attention to his dreams and seems often to have returned at night to the Germany he had left behind. On 15 November 1959 he noted down in his book a dream about Martin Buber:

> Dream. Long, very passionate conversation with Buber about Germany, about the laughable concept of honour, dueling and the like. I have forgotten all the details, except this I've retained. Buber said: "I have found refuge in the tranquillity of Germany philosophy." To which I – but now the scene had changed; he was standing in the street and I was leaning out of the window and calling out to him in a loud voice over the street noise – : "But younger people than you and even than me have to make a connection

with the proletariat." He listened to me very intently and endorsed what I'd said. Not just as if he'd heard it but as if he considered the thought particularly noteworthy too.

And years later Kraft wrote to Curd Ochwadt in Hanover:

By the way, I had a dream recently. We wanted to travel to Tel Aviv, but there were difficulties. Then suddenly war broke out. We ran. I saw, hidden in the corner, a *German* placard with this sentence on it: The mines have polluted our sacred Leine. Then I was returning books in the Bibliothèque Nationale in Paris, as if I didn't know that it's a reference-only library and I asked if I still hadn't handed in some books. A member of staff said in a friendly way: Yes, Constance von Borchardt. I nodded as if I were thinking this over. Then I said, but now another member of staff was sitting there, who was talking with a reader, in a heated and rather impolite way: Excuse me, a little mistake has occurred here. This has nothing to do with Constance von Borchardt. It's Armance von Stendhal. The staff member sat there with a stony face, as if I were air. Then I saw a third staff member, who was lying at full stretch on his table and telling what was evidently a very comical story to an acquaintance and I thought: people are like this here, while where we live there's a war. Then I woke up. Again I felt as if there were more genius in the dream itself than in all its interpretations.

He's right: these dreams speak for themselves. In the second, Kraft's three cities, Hanover, Paris and Jerusalem, all flow together into the river Leine. (The Leine flows through Hanover.) You could say that the political history he had repressed was returning twofold: abandoned, bygone Germany came back in Jerusalem's dreams.

In the Land of Israel: Ludwig Strauß

Rehavia was the neighbourhood of poets and thinkers. In the same house as Werner Kraft, 31 Alfasi Street, lived Ludwig Strauß, whom one might advisedly call a German-Jewish writer – because he was, as his editor Hans Otto Horch has shown, both at the same time: German and Jew. And he made this doubling into the essential theme of his work.

Born on 28 October 1892, scion of a Jewish merchant family in the old imperial city of Aachen, Ludwig was destined for the family business but prevailed against his parents' wishes and at Easter 1913 graduated from the humanistic gymnasium. In the same year, he began his studies on new literary history and philosophy in Berlin and met Martin Buber, who would have a determining influence on his work and career. Like many Jews of his generation, he expected the encounter with eastern Jewish culture to 'revolutionize the western Jewish intelligence'. Strauß wrote for German-Jewish magazines and translated from the Yiddish. In 1915 he was drafted into military service. He worked as a publisher's reader and as dramaturg at the Schauspielhaus in Düsseldorf, married Buber's daughter Eva and finally completed his doctorate with a thesis on Hölderlin and Schelling, supervised by Franz Schultz in Frankfurt am Main, who had granted Kraft his doctorate three years earlier. His habilitation followed in the next year, with a thesis on Hölderlin's 'Hyperion'. From 1929 Strauß taught at the technical college in his home city of Aachen. Alongside his teaching work he published stories, poems and essays.

Strauß made his first trip to Palestine in spring 1924 and returned to Germany profoundly affected by it. Ten years later, in late summer 1934 and under quite different omens, he scouted out work opportunities in the country and at the beginning of 1935 he resettled there, with his family following soon after. He worked at first at the Hasorea kibbutz and then from 1938 as an art and history teacher at the Ben Shemen Home for Children and Young People between Tel Aviv and Jerusalem. Shimon Peres, the Israeli politician-to-be, numbered among his pupils there.

Strauß produced his poem cycle *Land of Israel* in Palestine in 1934 and 1935 in the enthusiasm of arrival. Martin Buber, one of its first readers, believed that it would 'one day be valued as the quintessential lyrical expression of the German Aliyah', which is perhaps the most apt description of poems that allow us to see and read that new landscape through the eyes of German poetry. The seeing and the reading – of Israel's landscapes, of the Mediterranean, of the plains, of the Arabs and the Jewish settlers and the seasons – cannot be separated: it is the poetry of Hölderlin especially and even more of Stefan George that has sharpened our senses. The 'orange grove' takes on a mythic texture; the hot desert wind of the region, the 'Khamsin', becomes in these images an encounter with nature.

Strauß moved into 31 Alfasi Street in 1949, becoming Kraft's neighbour and close companion. He established comparative literature as a subject at the Hebrew University and wrote in German and Hebrew. Ludwig Strauß died on 11 August 1953.

From Merhavia to Rehavia: Tuvia Rübner

In 1941 the seventeen-year-old Tobias Rübner came from Pressburg (present-day Bratislava) to Merhavia, a place whose name has almost the same meaning as Rehavia. (As at the end of Psalms 118:5 (NIV): 'When hard pressed, I cried to the LORD; he brought me into a spacious place ["vam-mer-hav yah" in Hebrew]'). A play on words connects Rehavia in Jerusalem, the 'vastness of God', with the Merhavia kibbutz in the north of the country. Rübner's journey to Palestine took him through Hungary, Bulgaria, Turkey, Syria and Lebanon. Tobias, who called himself Tuvia from then on, never saw his parents and grandparents, his sister Alice or his childhood friends again. Spurred on to study Hebrew by his encounters with Werner Kraft and Ludwig Strauß, he became one of Israel's most significant poets. He translated S.Y. Agnon's *Shira* and the poems of Dan Pagis into German, and works by Kafka and Walter Benjamin into Hebrew. When the German Academy for Language and Literature elected him as a corresponding member, the new author introduced himself:

For twelve years after I came to that old, that new land, I wrote German poems. Most I made in my head, in a field with the sheep, whispering them to myself and only wrote them down once I was back in my room. [...] I wrote in a language I barely spoke any longer. That language was my home. In German I carried on speaking with my parents, with my sister, with my grandparents, relatives, my childhood friends, all of whom have no grave.

Around this time Rübner arrived at 31 Alfasi Street to meet Kraft, who had heard about the young poet. Between the older man and the shy young one a dialogue began that would last for decades, as Rübner recalls:

Werner Kraft died in 1991 and with him an era in my mental life came to an end. Every time I walked down the steps into his garden flat in the house at 31 Alfasi Street I was enriched. What remains from those many, many conversations on poetry, on Kafka, Benjamin, Goethe, Borchardt, on the current situation, on Jochmann, on new German poetry, on rhyme and on so much else, when I have noted none of it down? I see his bright eyes. I hear his childish laughter at some joke he has just told. [...] Werner Kraft was a poet of loyalty. He gave nothing up and he gave no ground: he remained loyal to his origins, his youth, to the poets who had formed his view of the world and they were all German. Loyalty did not forbid criticism, neither of the language, if it was incorrect, nor of those who spoke it. The scrupulous testing of his loyalty allowed him to write his series of monographs, as well as his entirely exceptional anthology *Rediscovery*, in which he gathered unknown work from known poets along with his new discoveries from the forgotten. He wrote in his minuscule handwriting almost to the end and it remained, almost to the end, clearly readable.

Rübner is right: Kraft remained loyal to Israel; in post-war Germany he would have been able to assert himself and his interests sooner, but the author himself, though more especially his wife and children, had long since put down roots in Jerusalem. 'Adamant' is a two-line poem, titled with an old, exquisite word for diamond:

I am unsound,
I give no ground.

Werner Kraft died in Jerusalem six weeks after his ninety-fifth birthday and was buried near the Tzova kibbutz, a half-hour from Jerusalem. His son-in-law Yoav Tibon and Tuvia Rübner spoke at the grave. Tuvia Rübner died at almost exactly the same age in summer 2019.

Heavenly Rehavia: Else Lasker-Schüler

Hebrew distinguishes between the upper and lower Jerusalem: it is the only city in the world which exists twice, in heaven and on Earth. 'If word went across Jerusalem that Rehavia had flown up into heaven overnight – it would not amaze me,' wrote Else Lasker-Schüler in her *Land of the Hebrews*, about her journey to Palestine in 1934. It is an account in which the earthly cannot be separated from the heavenly, nor the immanent from the transcendent. The gardens of Rehavia are also the Garden of Eden; the pious dwellings have wings to the rear for the journey to heaven; paperboys announce not only earthly news; past becomes present; the flowers neatly arrayed in the front gardens of Rehavia look like a toy in the long-lost home of her parents in Elberfeld, into which she was born, daughter of Jewish-Liberal citizens, in 1869. In 1894 she moved to Berlin with her first husband, Jonathan Berthold Lasker, learned to draw and joined a community of artists. She grew into a powerful and singular voice of literary modernism in the time of the Kaiser and still more in the Weimar Republic. In a magnificently free and unprecedentedly expansive way, Lasker-Schüler incorporates entire historical and biblical worlds into the smallest impressions of her trip to Palestine.

The poet set out to Palestine in 1934 and 1937, both times from her exile in Zürich. During her third and last trip, in 1939, the Swiss authorities forbade her to return 'on precautionary Poor Relief Policing grounds – Excess of Foreigners.'

Else Lasker-Schüler stayed at first at the Nordia Hotel, then the Vienna and the Atlantic on the arterial road, Jaffa Street. 'I often answer the question, why I do not live in Rehavia or some other suburb of Jerusalem, with an excuse – which is not wholly untrue: One can hardly eat only green dessert all day…' The poet knew herself well enough. In Zürich she had longed for Jerusalem; but barely had she arrived there than it seemed more desirable to be back in Zürich – to say nothing of Berlin. So, for years she did not move into her beloved colony.

I stroll along all by myself… across King George Street to Rehavia. I pass by the beautiful Yeshurun Synagogue and wonder whether I should climb the little hill of earth upon which that pious gem gleams and shimmers? Or should I make it in full to my objective, the home of the Keranoth

["Funds"] and the Jewish Agency? In my first book *Land of the Hebrews* I compared this wondrous building of the Hebrew Ministry to a rabboni who lovingly takes pilgrims into his arms. Built on the pattern of a half-moon, one believes from a distance that this superb structure is waning and waxing, effervescing red-yellow in the light of the evening hour. – In the entrance hall of this mighty palace, always guarding everyone in the same way, sits a delightful Jewish Man in the Moon. What a modest, bearded watchman! He knows already – that I want to go to my dear, tireless Geveret Kümmel…

Although Lasker-Schüler learned no more Hebrew and enrolled herself in her idiosyncratic English, she addressed almost everyone as 'Geveret' (Hebrew for 'Mrs') or 'Adon' ('Mr'). 'Geveret' Ryva Kimmel, who had arrived in Jerusalem from Berlin in 1936, worked in the German section of the Jewish Agency and looked after Lasker-Schüler's many needs. She arranged a pension for her, which the publisher Salman Schocken topped up, and she always had a sympathetic ear for the poet, who was not, as posterity's pious legend would have it, pauperised in Jerusalem but rather found support, encouragement and attention there. Shmuel Hugo Bergmann and his wife invited her over, as did the Agnons, the Kracauers, Leo and Grete Kestenberg and others. And one day the poet encountered the Bergmanns' neighbour in the house next door:

In the twin nests of the second building he grows wealthy off the teachings of the Kabbalah: Scholem, the renowned

Kabbalistic scholar. I visit by mistake, through no fault of my own – I got the wrong entrance. It doesn't seem to make the Kabbalist in his reading happy. I stay anyway! Taking abundant revenge on my persistence, Adon Scholem labours, with the toxins of logic, to pull down the legends of Holy Israel from the heavens for me. He concludes by uprooting the papyrus on which the first initials of our people were written. "When the miraculous enters into marriage with schoolmaster logic, the result is a *mésalliance*," I say. I toddle off indignantly. Some time after, however, our paths crossed again. We were both waiting at the stop for the omnibus to Jerusalem-City. We seated ourselves in the unoccupied places. Was my neighbour in a better humour? Or did nature, sighing with relief to be no longer clouded over by some dusty folio, have a favourable effect on his mood? Rejuvenated, he began to joke about our dispute, even though it had been religious; he had only wanted to test, he said, how far I was open to persuasion and proposed that we both of us cease to overheat ourselves over the life of our holy men. I gestured across the magnificent landscape – to our right and to our left and stretched myself up into the vault of heaven and assured this just-surfaced and youthful scholar, that I had learned the stories of our people's prophets from the book of heaven's own illustrated primer in its original printing.

Scholem for his part accused her of 'insanity'. His mother wrote to him that Lasker-Schüler's critique of Adon Scholem had 'thoroughly amused' her: 'I always found this little woman horrible & I do not understand how anyone can detect poetic art in her entirely senseless drivel.' What seemed like madness to some of her contemporaries was in truth what made Lasker-Schüler an exact chronicler of her mad times, in her portrayal of Nazism in her play *I-and-I* as much as in her appreciation of the political tensions and hardship in Palestine. Her money she gave away.

A thunderbolt flares in her eyes
And as the frenzy strives to break free,
She plunges again into life,
Gives secret noise to our griefs.
Our eyes open, our ears feast.

So wrote Werner Kraft in 'The Poetess'. Lasker-Schüler found an attentive public in Jerusalem. In September 1937 Erich Gottgetreu reports on a reading for the *Jüdische Presszentrale* ('Jewish Press Centre') newspaper in Zürich:

Else Lasker-Schüler spent some weeks in Zion. The romanticizing term is appropriate here. To her, Jerusalem is Zion, the 'fore-heaven to heaven'. This was her second stay in the Holy City, where the great Jewish poetess of the German tongue has many admirers. The Universitas bookshop exhibited a series of the poet's skillful drawings in honour of her distinguished visit. Dr. E. Lubrany discussed her oeuvre in the Hebrew hour on the radio. For us the highpoint was an evening performance at which Lasker-Schüler read from her work. It became apparent that the large guest room at the dairy, which stands in the villa district Rehavia opposite the Hebrew Gymnasium, could not hold her listeners. It looked like they needed a proper security cordon. Every so often another person would vault out onto the balcony and into the open window like a burglar.

The poet recited by candlelight from the Jerusalem chapter of *Land of the Hebrews*. The correspondent describes how the garden of the dairy and the balconies of the neighbouring houses filled up with people listening. He sees the heavenly events of the evening as the poetess might have: 'In the midst of the stars the moon hung crooked.'

Lasker-Schüler left thousands of letters and drawings – signed with her own name or as Prince Yusuf of Thebes – on sheets of paper, napkins and cards, often painted. Around 130 went to a neighbour in Rehavia: Ernst Simon. Born in Berlin in 1899, this early collaborator of Franz Rosenzweig and Martin Buber was led by the horror of the First World War to become a Zionist. He contributed to Buber's magazine *Der Jude* ('The Jew') and in 1928 emigrated to Palestine, where he soon became one of the country's pre-eminent educators. Lasker-Schüler, thirty years his senior, fell in love with Adon Simon and dedicated to him some of the most beautiful love poems in world literature. Her final volume of poetry, *My Blue Piano*, with its cycle 'To Him', includes 'A Love Song':

Come to me in the night – we'll sleep entwined.
I am so very tired, lonely from wakefulness.
In the dark dawn a strange bird sang,
as my dream still wrestled with itself, with me.

Around every spring the flowers are opening

and the immortelles are tinted by your eyes.

Come to me in the night, late into my tent,
in starflower shoes and cloaked in love.
Moons will rise from the heavens' dusty chests.

Like two rare beasts we will take love's rest
In the tall reeds behind this world.

When he received a copy of *My Blue Piano* in August 1943, the idolised and desired 'Apollon', 'You, cypress in Jerusalem', reacted with great nobility. He wrote to the poet: 'It will be my great honour to have served as the occasion for the most magnificent of poems. [...] Thus may I thank you for the book and kiss your hands. Your admiring and loyal, Ernst Simon.'

Lasker-Schüler's last book was published by the Tarshish publishing house in Rehavia, named after a place in the Bible known for its ships bearing precious cargo. Tarshish was the publishing house of Moshe Spitzer, who had been editor and designer of the famous Schocken Library and ultimately director of Schocken Verlag, based in Berlin until it was broken up in 1938. Today it is one of Israel's leading publishing houses. Lasker-Schüler wrote to Spitzer in 1943:

Adon! I am playing on my blue piano
A hymn of thanks to you for this!
in every tone.
Prince Yusuf

Her book was one of the last to be published in German in Jerusalem for a long time. The news from Germany from the fronts and especially the reports of the murder of the Jews in Eastern Europe reached Lasker-Schüler too. She struggled desperately to contact the Pope, Stalin or Emmy Göring. 'Every day can bring new murders,' she wrote in March 1943. The 'Kraal' she had gathered around herself in Rehavia to hold readings and lectures in German, and for which she had handwritten her invitations, scattered in all directions. Her last book she dedicated 'Loyally, to my not-to-be-forgotten friends in the cities of Germany – and those, like me, banished and now scattered in the world.'

In the end the eternal hotel guest did in fact move to Rehavia, taking a room on Ha-Ma'aloth Street with a cleaning-obsessed landlady. Frau Weidenfeld made life difficult for the poet. Lasker-Schüler's 'tender' mother, who had died young, returned in her last poems and letters, as did her son Paul, who had died in Berlin in 1927, aged just twenty-eight. In October 1944 she wrote to Ernst Simon in a rapture of 'Sie' (formal 'you') and 'Du' (informal 'you'):

I don't love *Dich* any more, Ernest, but it is some kind of gift for me, when I see *Sie*.[…] When I loved *Dich*, I had my own small secret paradise. We are only truly poor in our inner possessions. We can have no house, no palace, yet build from them a blue heaven. I am now entirely poor. But *Du*, Ernest, must remain forever Ernest, a boy more or less, but a happy one! *Du* dear boy. We would have eaten bonbons forever, even in our thoughts. But my heart can no longer speak to *Du*.

It's no fun being in Jerusalem. The mood is black. Rehavia has taken a hit. They have torn up something beautiful; it looks like after an earthquake – or during an earthquake. Great movements of people into the void. And today the manicured homes of Rehavia have been requisitioned by soldiers.

On the night of 29 November 1947 at Lake Success in America, two-thirds of the General Assembly of the United Nations voted for a plan to divide Palestine into two autonomous states. In the days that followed, an Arab general strike was called. The British Mandatory period ended on the night of 14 May 1948. David Ben-Gurion proclaimed the state of Israel. A minute after midnight the troops of the Arab armies invaded the country: Iraqi and Transjordanian soldiers from the east, units from Lebanon and Syria from the north. The Egyptian Air Force bombed Tel Aviv. The Arab Legion, commanded by British officers, seized the Jewish Old City and bombarded the Jewish areas of the city from the mountains circling Jerusalem, to induce the civilian population to capitulate. The ring around the city, the ring around Rehavia, tightened. Food became ever scarcer, the electricity supply ceased almost entirely, and water lorries drove through the streets, doling out a meagre ration to residents. The thunder of cannon fire could be heard day and night; few were the 'gun-silent hours' as Erich Gottgetreu, one of the chroniclers of Rehavia under siege, called them. One morning in May 1948 at half past four he dared to go out onto the street and marvelled:

Like our house, all the other houses in the Rehavia neighbourhood were still standing. Saw a few black gunshot holes in red roofs. Some debris in the gardens. A lacerated tree and, diagonally opposite our house, a shattered car. It belongs to Dr. Lachmann, who resignedly diagnosed the damage his expensive vehicle had sustained.

The university on Mount Scopus became an exclave, which could only be reached, perilously, by armoured convoy. Yet Gottgetreu was able to report:

The humanities academics among the university's scholars are busying themselves just the same with their research, in spite of all adversity, carrying on at domestic writing desks fortified with sandbags. Prof. Sukenik deciphers biblical texts over two thousand years old, written on leather scrolls; Bedouins found the scrolls in a cave by the Dead Sea before the outbreak of the war. And Prof. Torczyner continues with his great standard work on the birth and growth of the Hebrew language. Another works on problems in philosophy, history... Even here though there are interruptions, dictated by the emergency situation of these days. I saw the Egyptologist Prof. Polotsky employed as a water distributor, driving one of the water cars dispensing its blessings across the city – an apt image, since the prudent distribution of water was an Ancient Egyptian science.

During this time a celebration took place, as Felix Weltsch reported to Max Brod on 15 February 1948:

A couple of days ago was the 70th birthday party for Buber at [Werner] Senator's. Strange, there was not one Hebr. word! Much was said, the most significant by Scholem, who in his amiable way told Buber that in truth he had failed at everything. But that this was exactly what Scholem liked about him. Buber wanted precisely not to be an "easy to handle Rabbi", as people demanded of him. (By the way, amiable to me as well: He suddenly asked in the middle of his speech: Where is the auth. Buber generation among the three speech givers? Where is Prague? At which someone points at me: "He's sitting there." To which Scholem: "Exactly, he's sitting.") Buber seized on the failure: yes, that's right, but through that – "through failure we grow". This seemed a pretty banal doctrine to me, even if it's mine too: as Rottenstreich immediately remarked: Well! *You* are probably satisfied with Buber today!

Even under bombardment, in spite of curfews and short-ages, intellectual dispute remained Rehavia's elixir of life.

A Birthday in Jerusalem: Martin Buber and Baruch Kurzweil

In February 1963, Rehavia assembled to celebrate Martin Buber's eighty-fifth birthday just as it had gathered around him in 1948 for his seventieth – and the same chronicler recorded:

[The] usual liter. grandees with their spouses, inc. Agnon, Bergmann, Simon, Scholem, Kraft, Prof. Zondek,

Schereschwesky, Spitzer, Meier and others, as well as Buber's family and Kurzweil from TA. (The latter then involuntarily ensured that he lived up to his name [Kurzweil = "amusement" or "pastime"]).

Felix Weltsch was reporting to Max Brod again about the birthday party, in which everyone sat together in the central room of Buber's house.

Simon delivers a very handsome address, genial and humorous, memories from the days of the magazine *Der Jude* ["The Jew"]. Then Kurzweil gives his speech, good and softly spoken, full of warmth and appreciation for Buber. Only then the "conversation" begins; and the theme was… Kafka! Buber defended his conception of Kafka against the critique which Kurzweil had published to mark Buber's birthday in *Haaretz* and *MB*. The focus was on the naturally not new question of whether Kafka was a religious nihilist or whether he nevertheless believed, beyond the desolation and impenetrable in-between layer of bureaucracy, in an existing transcendence. Buber says yes, Kurzweil no. Buber invokes his well-known essay, in which he defends the "ontic" character of guilt via a condemnation of the psychoanalyt. position (here I entirely agree with him) and read out, with great difficulty, using a strong magnifying glass, the aphorism 'Stand facing the rain…' which evidently he had now copied out for himself […]. Kurzweil's response was harsh and fierce: A writer's aphorisms have no role to play in the interpretation of his work, just as little as his diaries and letters. The novel has to speak for itself and it is clearly nihilistic. Buber disagrees. The well-known controversy has arrived: the literary critic will not allow the theologian to interfere in his work, nor the ontologist the psychologist. Scholem says something on the subject, in line with Buber, also a little of his own view and now Kurzweil becomes thoroughly harsh and coarse. He rages in a delicate voice.

A birthday among scholars. At its heart is conversation, no matter how disputatious.

Buber however was absolutely not tired and made a lively impression both physically and mentally. Also: the interesting point was that at a party for Buber people spoke almost the whole time about Kafka and that Kurzweil, prince of literature, did not restrain his belligerence for the sake of the party atmosphere or the expressions on people's faces.

In its discussion of Kafka's work and how to interpret and understand it existentially, historically, politically, theologically or psychoanalytically, Jerusalem was not so far removed from Prague, the home city of Weltsch and Brod and home area of Baruch Kurzweil. Three months later the famous Kafka Conference took place in Liblice, partly initiated by Eduard Goldstücker, Czechoslovakia's first ambassador to Israel from 1950 to 1951. The discussions among the Czech and Slovak writers and literary scholars smoothed the path for the Prague Spring. Quarrelsome Kurzweil was one of the most influential literary critics in Israel. Born in 1907 in Moravia, he trained as a rabbi in Frankfurt am Main and studied German language and literature. In 1933 he completed his doctorate with a thesis on Goethe's *Faust* and worked as a teacher at the Jewish Gymnasium in Berlin, before he emigrated to Palestine in 1939. In 1955 he became professor at the newly founded Bar-Ilan University. Some years after this memorable birthday party Kurzweil was supposed to be invited to Frankfurt. Theodor W. Adorno made inquiries with Scholem about the prospective visitor: 'Kurzweil is thought of as "difficult" too, which can as easily speak in his favour as against him.' Scholem replied by return mail to Frankfurt that Kurzweil was paranoid about him and had been for years tirelessly writing essays 'in which he [presents] me as a nihilist, demonologist, associate of quasi-Nazis (Eranos!!), evangelist (!!!) for myth, secularist, a slave to provincial ideas and secularist Zionism'. Kurzweil's criticism was defined not only by literature but also, strongly, by the tenets of Orthodox Judaism. The quarrelsome critic was not invited to Frankfurt.

Geography of the Soul: Lea Goldberg

When the *Frankfurter Allgemeine Zeitung* published a poem by Lea Goldberg on 30 November 1990, translated from the Hebrew by Tuvia Rübner, only a few readers would have known who the poet was. And yet this poem, by Goldberg, born 1911 in Königsberg and raised in Russia and Lithuanian Kovno (now Kaunas), offers a rarely equalled witness to the experience of emigration. It speaks of becoming aware of your origins in a moment of your life, of a lost and unreachable homeland of landscapes and seasons, of being rooted there and putting down roots here. For all this, Goldberg coined the phrase 'geography of the soul', which incorporates the external into the inward and allows the inward to be seen and to be read:

> Here I cannot hear the voice of the cuckoo.
> Here the tree will never wear a cape of snow.
> But it is here in the shade of these pines
> my entire childhood comes alive.
>
> The chime of the needles: Once upon a time –
> I called the snow-space homeland,
> and the green ice that enchains the stream,
> and the poem's tongue in a foreign land.
>
> Perhaps only migrating birds know –
> suspended as they are between earth and sky –
> this heartache of two homelands.
>
> With you I was transplanted twice,
> with you, pine trees, I grew,
> my roots in two different lands.

If *Haaretz* had published the poem – original title, 'Ilanot' ('Pines') – most if not all its readers would have known its author. Goldberg is the best-known lyric poet in Israel. Giddon Ticotsky has brought out a new edition of her novels, stories and poems; there are films about her, exhibitions of her drawings and sound recordings. In German there are her novels *Letters from an Imaginary Journey* and *Losses*, and some of her poems in a translation by Gundula Schiffer. Rachel Tzvia Back has translated her poetry into English.

For many years Goldberg lived at 16 Alfasi Street, a few houses away from Werner Kraft and Ludwig Strauß. As a city, Tel Aviv moulded Lea Goldberg and her writing. In 1955 she moved to Jerusalem and taught literature at the Hebrew University, in the footsteps of Strauß. Meiser Hall, a large auditorium, could barely hold the number of students who flocked to her lectures on the Russian novel, Dante, Rilke and modern Hebrew literature. The author Chaim Be'er describes in the film *In the Five Houses* how he once travelled on the same bus, the 405 bus from Jerusalem to Tel Aviv, as Goldberg, who was smoking and leaning out of the window. After they arrived in Tel Aviv, he followed her to see where his teacher was actually going. She took the same bus back to Jerusalem. When he told this story to his friend T. Carmi, himself also later a significant author and publisher, Carmi offered the theory that the restlessness of travelling – Goldberg travelled all across Europe as well, though no longer to Germany – was the mode of living best suited to her.

> White days, as long as the sun's rays in summer.
> Loneliness rests a long time on the river's breadth.
> Windows stand wide open in sky-blue hush.
> The bridges between yesterday and tomorrow are straight
>   and tall.

This bridge-building poem was written in Hebrew in Bonn in 1932 and was first published in Kovno, and then soon after in Goldberg's first book in Tel Aviv. Yfaat Weiß has written about Lea Goldberg's apprentice years in Germany between 1930 and 1933, her path from Kovno via Bonn to

Berlin, where she studied and gained her doctorate. With *Letters from an Imaginary Journey* she bade farewell to Berlin, which she would not see again.

For her first translations from Lithuanian into Hebrew, the eighteen-year-old Goldberg chose the telling pseudonym 'Lea Meshorer' ('Lea Poet'). This name leads us to one of her key works, her essay 'Encounter with a Poet'. The poet in question is Avraham Ben Yitzhak, originally Avraham Sonne, the subject of Elias Canetti's chapter 'Dr Sonne' in his memoirs of Vienna in the 1930s. Goldberg's essay describes Ben Yitzhak's poetics, which includes his life, his power of judgement, something of his brevity, which eschewed the feeling of depth in favour of depth itself, the many languages he mastered, his modesty and his slender body of work – an oeuvre which amounted in all to just twelve poems, the best known being 'Blessed are they that sow and do not reap'. Sonne, born in Galicia in 1883, first set out to Jerusalem as early as 1913, but had an accident en route and returned to Vienna. In the 1920s he studied Hebrew in Vienna, surrounded by a circle of friends and supporters such as Arthur Schnitzler, Arnold Schönberg, James Joyce, Hermann Broch and Canetti himself, on whom Ben Yitzhak had a lasting influence. Canetti wrote: 'Nothing that Sonne spoke of was thereby done with or settled. It was more interesting than before, it was organized and illuminated. He laid out entire lands in one stroke, where before there had been only dark but questioning points.'

In 1938 Sonne fled Vienna for Jerusalem, where he took the name Ben Yitzhak. And there Goldberg encountered him. She understood brilliantly how to seize on seemingly small episodes, which the poet narrated to her or which she experienced with him herself, about a performance of *Every-man* in Salzburg, or the workshop of a Viennese shoemaker in Jerusalem, or his pronunciation of the word 'Krieg' ('war'), or a bunch of violets, which Lea Goldberg presented to Else Lasker-Schüler in Café Sichel. Every image or scene had its own particular historical signature and this encounter with another poet was often the self-encounter of Lea Goldberg with Lea Meshorer as well.

Eichmann in Rehavia: Hannah Arendt

At the beginning of Margarethe von Trotta's film *Hannah Arendt*, the title character is engrossed in conversation with an older friend. They are discussing Adolf Eichmann, who at the time of the scene is in custody in Israel, having been abducted in Argentina a year earlier. Eichmann was a Lieutenant Colonel (Obersturmbannführer) in the SS and director of the 'Jewish Section' in the Reich Security Main Office, responsible for the deportation of hundreds of thousands of Jews to concentration camps and death camps. As we now know, Fritz Bauer, the attorney general of Hesse, and his Israeli colleague Chaim Cohn, born in Lübeck, played a significant role in Eichmann's capture: the one by bypassing the reluctant German authorities, the other by mobilising his country's secret service, Mossad.

Eichmann's trial began on 11 April 1961 with hundreds of journalists in attendance, both from Israel and abroad, and the proceedings were broadcast directly on the radio not only in West Germany but also in the GDR. The trial brought enormous attention to the fate of Europe's Jews in the twelve years of Nazism and became a forum for discussion in the young state of Israel and in post-war German society. In Israel, as Raphael Gross says, the trial strengthened the collective identification with the Holocaust. The presiding judge, Moshe Landau, his associate judges and the state prosecutor had all studied in Germany.

Hannah Arendt travelled to Jerusalem to observe the trial for the *New Yorker* – and met up with her old friend Kurt Blumenfeld. The scene in the 2012 film was shot on the terrace of the Scottish Church on the border of Abu Tor and the German Colony. It could have been a café in Rehavia. Arendt stayed at first in the Hotel Moriah on King George Street, then at the Pension Reich in Beit Hakerem, the western city district, and often in Tel Aviv, where her cousin Ernst Fürst lived with his wife, Käthe. Blumenfeld and Arendt knew each other from the Berlin of the early 1930s, when she had been part of a circle of Zionists, whom she now re-encountered in Jerusalem: Robert Weltsch and Siegfried Moses. With Blumenfeld she shared a common homeland in East Prussia and memories that went back a long way; she had met her friend, twenty-two years her senior, in Heidelberg at a meeting of Zionist students. After a long evening, Blumenfeld became her 'mentor in political matters', but at the same time she loved his free spirit and playfulness. Their friendship revived when they re-encountered each other in Jerusalem in 1961.

She had first met Gershom Scholem in Jerusalem in 1935, while she was accompanying a group of young immigrants to Palestine. In October 1940 she had sent him the news: 'Dear Scholem – Walter Benjamin has taken his own life, on 26.9., on the Spanish border, in Portbou,' concluding with: 'Jews are dying in Europe and they are burying them like dogs.'

After fifty-six days of hearing evidence, including testimonies from many survivors, the District Court in Jerusalem sentenced Adolf Eichmann to death. The accused and his defence lawyer Servatius lodged an appeal, but the Supreme Court confirmed the sentence in May 1962. In the end the Israeli President, Yitzhak Ben-Zvi, rejected Eichmann's plea for mercy. Before that, the representatives of Rehavia – Martin Buber, Gershom Scholem, Shmuel Hugo Bergmann, Ernst Simon and Chaim Cohn – had argued against carrying out the sentence in a submission to the president. On 31 May 1962 the sentence of death was carried out.

When Arendt's famous book *Eichmann in Jerusalem* appeared the following year, its firmly expressed criticism of how the Jewish representatives in the camps, the so-called Judenräte ('Jewish Councils'), had collaborated with the German command in the concentration camps and ghettos triggered a fierce reaction in Israel but above all in the USA. On 23 June 1963 Scholem wrote to Arendt:

I find in your exposition of this Jewish behaviour under extreme circumstances, which neither of us experienced, no carefully considered judgement but rather overstatement degenerating often into demagoguery. Who of us today can say what decisions those Jewish Elders, or whatever one wants to call them, should have taken under the circumstances of that time? I do not know and I have read no less than you on the subject. From your analyses I do not gain the impression that your knowing is better than my unknowing. [...] I do not presume to judge. I was not there.

She believed, Arendt responded, 'that we will only be able to deal with this past if we begin to make judgements, even strong ones. I have expressed my judgement in this case clearly but evidently you have not understood it. There was no possibility of resistance, but there was the possibility of doing nothing.' Scholem had accused her of lacking 'ahabath Israel' ('love of the Jewish people'). 'You are absolutely right, that I have no such love,' Arendt advised him:

> ... and this on two grounds: First, I have never in my life loved any people or collective, neither the Germans, nor the French, nor the Americans, nor some kind of Working Class or whatever else of this tariff. In fact I love only my friends and I am entirely incapable of any other love. Second, moreover, this kind of love would be suspect to me, since I myself am Jewish.

The friendship between Arendt and Scholem, if it ever was that, ended eventually in silence. Thanks to the annotated correspondence assembled by Marie Luise Knott and David Heredia, we know today how intensively the two of them collaborated to salvage Jewish cultural assets in the devastated Europe of 1945. In the years of enforced separation letters from friends were, as Arendt wrote in 1942, 'like very thin, strong threads, with which you want to persuade yourself that it might still be possible to bind together the remnants of our world.'

'So, until we meet again, perhaps!' wrote Scholem to Arendt in what seems to be his last letter to her. They did not meet again, and the disagreement remained profound between the political philosopher Arendt and the historian and philologist Scholem, who had adopted Aby Warburg's saying as his motto, that our dear God is in the detail. The devil and the banality of evil too. In any case, Arendt's friends in Rehavia and many in New York turned their backs not just on her book and its theses but on her. In May 1963 she travelled to Jerusalem again to say her farewells to Blumenfeld, who lay on his deathbed. Half a century later, her great-niece Edna Brocke told the story:

> I brought her to the home where Blumenfeld was being looked after. But I did not fetch her back as well: she came back to our house in a taxi. I will never forget the sight. They had not let her go to him. She sat at our dining table, hunched over herself and was silent for the longest time...

In *Eichmann in Jerusalem* Arendt failed to give her readers the 'very old-fashioned, objective and exhaustive treatment' of historical conditions that Scholem had demanded from her – as we know today after decades of intensive research. But her friends too, those who turned their backs on her, failed to give Arendt what she had demanded of Scholem years earlier in another dispute: 'namely, that a person is worth more than their opinions, for the simple reason that people are de facto more than what they think and do'.

'Homeland – What Number are You?'
Mascha Kaléko in Jerusalem

On 29 August 1963 Mascha Kaléko wrote to a friend in New York:

> In a café here (café – slight euphemism in Jerusalem) I met a woman doctor from Berlin, who I knew at a distance in my student years. She looked so lonely that I went right up to her and told her that she looked nice. As it happens, it was true, and I just grabbed the bull by the horns, so to speak. She beamed at my sincere compliment and I said: it's the truth and I don't understand why all the truths we have to tell people are uncomfortable ones. A little later she came over to my table and said that she wanted to say something pleasing to me too. She showed me a small antique object, which she said she had just received from Paris. She took pleasure in my admiration for this gift, which a beloved relative had sent to her. I told this story to my Vinaver and said that I had the feeling she was very lonely and there are so many lonely people in this city and actually we ought to be looking after them. But I'm such a bad looker-after. And 2 days later I read a death notice for this (57-year-old) woman, who really did look good and was charming and intelligent and a cancer research specialist. Apparent suicide, as they say. I can be as fatalist as you like – but somewhere inside the feeling of guilt lingers.

This episode says a great deal about Kaléko: her Berliner turns of phrase, her empathy and gentle self-deprecation, and the apparently casual style, which tells us a great deal about the tragedy of an individual person, a story about history and place.

Kaléko had moved to Jerusalem from New York in October 1959 with her husband Chemjo Vinaver, a composer of Hasidic music, in the hope that Vinaver's severe asthma would be alleviated by the city's dry, mountain climate. But the climate quickly proved more and more malignant for them both as the years passed. These 'escapees from New York' lived at first on Balfour Street, then moved to Gaza Street before ending up at 33 King George Street in 1962:

> Instead of a provincial style building with just a few tenants and a little patch of garden, which is the norm here, we have been forced, because nothing else was available and "affordable" right now, to rent on the 7th floor of a sky-scraper (which in fact only "scrapes" seven floors high). But I do see the pluses: no neighbours above us except the – here – splendidly starry sky. And a view out over old Jerusalem, with its ancient past, as closed to us as "East Berlin" is to you. But from the 7th floor we can see over the dangerous city walls beyond to Jordan. The part of Jerusalem in which the Jews are allowed to live is alas horribly disfigured by new buildings, which undoubtedly take account of the need to house the population, but exude nothing of the spirit of the Old City...

When Kaléko first arrived in Jerusalem she was amazed that complete strangers were addressing her by her first name, until, after a while, she established that 'ma ha-sha'a' means 'What time is it?' in Hebrew. She never gained a more secure footing in Jerusalem. The city remained foreign to her, even once she'd made friends or maintained friendships with Rehavites like Gerda and Hermann Zondek, Sonja and Erich Gottgetreu, the Kupferbergs, Suse Weltsch, all of them from Berlin. At the end of 1955 Kaléko set out on her first trip to Germany. She stayed some weeks in a wintry Hamburg and then travelled to her home city.

> Berlin, in March. My first Germany trip,
> since they banished me a millennium ago.
> I see the city in a new way,
> with the foreigner's guidebook in my hand.
> The sky turns blue. The pines rustle softly.
> Yesterday in Steglitz a tit spoke to me
> in the Schloßpark. It recognized me.

So runs the first verse of her 'Reunion with Berlin'. There she rediscovers her sister Lea, two years her junior, whom she had believed dead. And she witnesses Rowohlt Verlag's republication of her first book, *The Lyrical Shorthand Notebook*, originally published in January 1933. The rise of Nazism had soon led to a complete ban on the dissemination of her lyrics, but she was still able to publish *A Short Primer for Grown-Ups* in 1934, a book of poems. In their concision, local colour and melancholy touched with euphoria, the poems could only have originated in Berlin, where they were declared 'shameful and undesirable literature'. And this time? In the first three months of 1956, the republished *Shorthand Notebook* sold over 40,000 copies. Kaléko was invited to bookshops and libraries, TV and radio stations. She and Gottfried Benn struck up a friendship. 'Berliners have a beating heart beneath that famously gruff exterior,' she wrote in May 1956 to her publisher Ledig-Rowohlt: 'Some of them write to me, hoping that I might find a home here again, when alas the Berlin which I *am still seeking* no longer exists.' Kaléko stayed seven months in Berlin and returned for another long stay in her home city in 1958.

Born 7 June 1907 in Chrzanów in Galicia, Golda Malka, called Mascha, moved with her family to Germany in 1914. As a Russian national her father was interned on the outbreak of the First World War. After stays in Frankfurt am Main and Marburg, the family finally settled in Berlin. Mascha left the Jewish Girls' School with only her school certificate. She began a clerical apprenticeship in the offices of the Jewish Workers' Relief organisation and audited classes in philosophy and psychology at Berlin's Friedrich Wilhelm University and Lessing Gymnasium. Later she attended courses on advertising, which would shape her lyrics with their attentiveness to what lies close at hand, to everyday routine, and their catchy rhymes and images.

Kaléko was first in Palestine in 1935; in spring 1938 she visited her parents and siblings, who had immigrated there, in Tel Aviv. She knew the country; but for Kaléko, her husband and their son Steven, born in Berlin in 1936, the emigration route that would save their lives led them to New York. In 1949 Ledig-Rowohlt visited the poet in New York and tried to bring her to reissue her work, but she refused to publish in Germany. Seven years later when she nevertheless did so, she experienced a comeback like no other emigrant author on their return to Germany. She was popular in the truest sense of the word; her readers, especially her male readers, were attentive; she was invited everywhere. Yet in 1959 she turned her back not only on New York but on Berlin as well, no doubt mostly for the sake of her husband but also because she herself no longer felt truly on solid ground there. In the year of her move to Jerusalem she withdrew her candidacy for the Fontane Prize from the Academy of Arts in Berlin, as it had been awarded to her by Hans Egon Holthusen, the director of the academy's poetry section and a member of the prize jury. She declared to the greatly embarrassed gentlemen of the academy:

> It simply goes against the grain for me to receive a prize from the hands of a former SS man. However much any author might welcome the laurels and the tinkling coins associated with such an honour – as both an author and a Jew I can receive nothing from such a hand.

Their General Secretary, Baron von Buttlar, sprang to his feet. 'I am not a Jew and I have been through at least as much as the Jews. – But one cannot hold a youthful indiscretion like being a member of the SS against Holthusen for all eternity.' Kaléko noted down the scene for posterity; at the time the public learned nothing of the quarrels over the rejected prize.

Interest in Kaléko and her work grew quieter in the 1960s. Thanks to Jutta Rosenkranz's edition of the complete works, we have since 2012 known Kaléko as a wonderful letter writer, precise in image and rich in irony, especially towards herself. On her trips she sent long letters to her husband almost daily, providing almost a chronicle of everyday life in post-war

Germany. 'This is indeed Krähwinkel [a fictional town, epitomising provincial bourgeois narrow-mindedness] with branches all over the world,' she wrote (in English) of the Jerusalem in which she lived to a female friend in New York. To another: 'I can't speak good Ivrit [Hebrew] but I could say "All is vanity" in Ivrit back long before I had even thought of Israel…' Berlin casts images of longing across her poems and letters. Barbara Schopplick, a young Berliner, sent to Kaléko in Jerusalem roses and newspaper clippings, 'Berlin things (thanks to which I long for Berlin almost more than I did before, or at least for that particular Berlin that was my Berlin, and which even today – when I'm there – reaches me here and there and greets me, as if from another world).' And in a letter from March 1964 she included a poem:

Last night I woke up with these lines, which came to me not by chance:

"Tomorrow," I say. "Tomorrow."
"The day after tomorrow" even.
Now life is over,
And "tomorrow" never was.

When the Six Day War broke out in June 1967, Kaléko and her husband in Zürich were afraid for a Jerusalem under threat: 'HOW ARE YOU and YOUR CHILDREN, answer please, and do it on a postcard. What are the Zondeks and all our friends doing?' On 20 June 1967 Kaléko wrote to her lawyer in Berlin, Ernst-Ludwig Fischer: 'I wrote "Homeland, what number are you?" in New York. Now my "homeland number whatever" is gone too, it seems, even if our home is still standing…'

Kaléko's son, Steven, worked as a theatre director in the USA, seldom contacted her and hardly ever came to Jerusalem. He seems rather to have sought closeness with his father, but in all probability he was also concealing what both parents may have guessed but never expressed: that Steven was homosexual. In July 1968 the thirty-one-year-old fell ill with pancreatitis during rehearsals. His mother travelled to Pittsfield in Massachusetts. Steven died on 28 July 1968. From this calamity his parents never recovered. Kaléko and Vinaver travelled without resting back and forth between Jerusalem and Europe. In December 1973 Vinaver became seriously ill and died in Tel Aviv. Kaléko read one more time on 16 September 1974 at the America Memorial Library at Hallesches Tor in Berlin, not far from her familiar territory. 'A Street Named Bleibtreu' originates from this time (Kaléko lived on Bleibtreustraße in Berlin; 'bleibtreu' literally means 'stay faithful'):

Almost forty years ago I lived here.
… Something tugs at my sleeve, as I
amble – that's probably the word –
the length of Kurfürstendamm.
And I intended to look for nothing.
And again and again the tugging.
Be reasonable, I say to her.
Forty years! I'm not what I was.
Forty years. How often have my cells
renewed themselves in the meantime

on foreign land, in exile.
New York, Ninety-Sixth Street and Central Park,
Minetta Street in Greenwich Village.
And Zürich and Hollywood. And then still Jerusalem…

Mascha Kaléko died on 21 January 1975 in Zürich. Whoever seeks her traces in Jerusalem will find them in Berlin.

Arrival of the Chancellor: Konrad Adenauer

At the beginning of May 1966 a long-awaited guest from Germany arrived in Rehavia: ninety-year-old Konrad Adenauer, former Chancellor of West Germany and Honorary Chairman of the CDU (Christian Democratic Union), had made the trip from Bonn to Israel. David Ben-Gurion had invited him long before, when he was Adenauer's opposite number, at New York's Waldorf Astoria and had been able to come to an agreement with the then Chancellor over Germany's reparations for the Holocaust. Adenauer's visit was politically sensitive, as he was a high-ranking German politician of the Federal Republic making an official visit to the Jewish nation state. True, Theodor Heuss, former President of West Germany, had already visited, since Heuss, closely tied to Buber, had taken a strong interest in Israel during his presidency (1949–1959), as had the Bundestag President, Eugen Gerstenmaier. But the Israeli government classed both men as 'of clean record' with regard to their biographies between 1933 and 1945, and anyway both were more figureheads than real political actors. Adenauer by contrast was still an active politician. He had resolutely led the negotiations between

Germany and Israel since the early 1950s, had reluctantly ceded the chancellery to Ludwig Erhard just two-and-a-half years earlier and had given up the leadership of his party barely six weeks before his trip. And his Chief of Staff in the chancellery for many years, Hans Globke, now in retirement, had written supportive legal commentary on the Nuremberg Race Laws. Following the establishment of diplomatic relations between the two states the previous year, Adenauer's visit, attended by fierce protests from the Israeli population, had a high symbolic power.

The old master knew this well and worked through his first engagements – the award of an honorary doctorate at the Weizmann Institute in Rehovot and a press conference – as straight as an arrow. But on the evening of the first day of his visit in Jerusalem, in Rehavia to be precise, the acrimony began. *Der Spiegel* reported in May 1966 on the dinner that Israeli Prime Minister Levi Eshkol gave for Adenauer and his entourage:

> The festive gleam of the candles decorating Levi Eshkol's dining table fell on angry faces. Every time the brown sliding door which separated off the dining room of the Israeli Prime Minister's modest residence at 44 Ben Maimon Boulevard opened a crack those honoured guests still persevering in the living room saw that Konrad Adenauer's first banquet on Israeli soil was proceeding rather as though it would be his last. Eshkol had summoned 17 prominent representatives, Strauß's arms trading partner Shimon Peres among them, for nine o'clock on Tuesday evening last week to pay their respects to the Chancellor of

the reparations. By ten o'clock, however, they had already seen the sweat-soaked German Ambassador Pauls and visibly ill-at-ease Israeli Foreign Minister Abba Eban temporarily leave their host's circle of guests. Because within there was something sour for dessert. Quite inadvertently, yet for that reason all the more painfully, it had become apparent once again how the irresolvable entanglements of the past and the unresolved problems of the present shape the coexistence of Jews and Germans more strongly than the goodwill which Konrad Adenauer had been invited to demonstrate and for which he had come.

Levi Eshkol had turned to Adenauer in his after-dinner speech and declared 'that the Reparations Agreement which you have signed in the name of your people is not an atonement; that there is no atonement for such atrocities, no atonement for such annihilation'. He added: 'The Jewish people are waiting for further signs and tokens that the German people recognize the dreadful burden of the past and seek for themselves a new path among the family of peoples.' Adenauer, who wanted to have found that path long ago, responded, visibly angry: 'If goodwill goes unrecognized, nothing good can come of it.' Eshkol attempted to mollify his infuriated guest, saying that he considered Adenauer to be 'pointing the way ahead on this path' – a compliment – but the Chancellor responded: 'Mr Prime Minister, what you think is of no concern to me and how you rate me does not interest me in the slightest. I represent the German people. You have insulted them and for that reason I will be leaving tomorrow morning.' And then he requested Ambassador

Pauls to arrange the plane for the flight home. What Dan Diner identified as the 'ritualised distance' at the first meeting between Israelis and a German governmental commission in 1952 at Wassenaar in the Netherlands – the careful separation, formality and ordering of conversation – had led fourteen years later to definitive distance, to a 'dreadful row', as the former Chancellor later described it.

Only with difficulty was Nahum Goldmann able to placate Adenauer, late that evening of 3 May 1966 back at the King David Hotel. Over the following days, the former Chancellor carried out the rest of his planned programme: he laid a black, red and gold wreath at Yad Vashem, spoke with Israeli President Zalman Shazar and delivered a speech at the Hebrew University in the midst of furious student protests. The German ambassador, Rolf Pauls, held a reception at the Sheraton Hotel in Tel Aviv, which Mascha Kaléko attended. Adenauer travelled to Haifa as well and into the north of the country and finally made a friendly, intimate visit to David Ben-Gurion at the Sde Boker kibbutz, the photos from which later went around the world. Goldmann, as President of the World Jewish Congress, made up for things in an address two days later, in a way the guest from Germany seems to have considered appropriate: 'This legislation for reparations and restitution is a unique phenomenon.'

It is no coincidence that this clash in Jerusalem took place in the same year that the World Jewish Congress, under its President, Goldmann, invited participants to a forum in Brussels entitled 'Jews and Germans – an unresolved problem'. The diverse speakers at the August 1966 event spoke in widely varying registers. Bundestag President Eugen Gerstenmaier (as Gershom Scholem later wrote) 'invoked the borders of a patient and respectful distance between Germans and Jews and yet nonetheless concluded with a plea for a "stormproof normality between our two peoples".' In his welcome address, the philosopher Karl Jaspers spoke of the responsibility of citizens for the behaviour of the states in which they live. Golo Mann expressed grief and scepticism; after what had happened, he would never again be able to trust his own people, the Germans. The historian Salo W. Baron highlighted Christianity's anti-Jewish traditions. And Scholem concluded his historically lucid and wide-ranging speech with the question 'Where now do we stand, after the unspeakable horror of those twelve years?' Understanding between Germans and Jews depends on what language they are able or not able to find, he said, as the collision between two politicians in Rehavia three months earlier had so eloquently attested: 'Only in being mindful of this past, which we will never fully penetrate, can a new hope germinate for the restoration of speech between Germans and Jews and the reconciliation of those who have been separated.'

Self-Displaced Person: Peter Szondi

As his Swiss Air flight from Zürich landed at Lod Airport on 24 January 1968, Peter Szondi was leaving a restive and roiling West Berlin behind him. Since the murder of the young man Benno Ohnesorg by a police officer the year before, the student revolt had grown ever fiercer. Lectures were being disrupted and seminars broken up; the Institute for General and Comparative Literature, which Szondi had founded in 1965, had been directly affected. Now the thirty-eight-year-old was taking up an invitation to Jerusalem, arranged by Gershom Scholem and delivered by Lea Goldberg.

Scholem had encountered Szondi some years earlier:

> I hear by the way that a young Hungarian Jew, now a Swiss, whom I met 6 weeks ago in Zürich, wants to gain his habilitation with a paper or lecture on Walter Benjamin at the West's University in Berlin. His name is Peter Szondi and he seems not unintelligent. But what an irony! A Jew gains his habilitation at a post-Hitler German university with a paper on a man who himself could not earn his habilitation at a German university with any paper at all.

So wrote Scholem in November 1960 to Ernst Schoen, a childhood friend of Walter Benjamin. Szondi did in fact deliver his inaugural lecture as professor the following year on 'The Search for Lost Time in Walter Benjamin'. He had made his name with his *Theory of the Modern Drama* in 1956 and followed it with *An Essay on the Tragic* and work on Hölderlin, Celan, the questions of poetic genre and essays on Walter Benjamin, whose writings he had discovered back in 1949 in Zürich's Social Archives with his childhood friend Ivan Nagel.

Born in 1929 in Budapest, Szondi managed in December 1944, along with his parents, the psychiatrist Leopold Szondi and his wife Lilo, and his sister Eva-Vera, to get out of the Bergen-Belsen concentration camp into exile in Switzerland on the so-called Kasztner train. (Rezsö Kasztner – or Rudolf Kastner – as a representative of the Hungarian Jews, managed to negotiate with Adolf Eichmann for the safe passage of over sixteen hundred Jews in return for money and valuables of strategic worth to the German armed forces.)

Szondi's arrival in Jerusalem in January 1968 was linked to Benjamin's abortive journey forty years earlier, which must have come up frequently between Scholem and Szondi. There was no possibility of making good on Benjamin's trip now, but Szondi followed in its tracks. He taught Israeli students European literature, including German literature, in English and French – though certainly not in German – and took lodgings in Rehavia.

Scholem had written to Szondi at the beginning of January 1968 that he had 'reserved a relatively large room with bathroom and half board (without is not possible)… in the Wolff Guest House directly opposite us on Abarbanel Street from 24th January to 1st March' and after that 'booked a tiny suite, comprising two little rooms and a bathroom, likewise with half board, at the second guest house… called Grete Ascher, (the house right next to ours)'. And he added: 'Our neighbourliness and good character will perhaps compensate you for the drawbacks of guest house existence. You may also expect to receive a sandwich provided by us if you have the inclination.'

Szondi wrote no letters during his weeks in Israel and no record of his stay by him survives. Scholem, however, wrote at the end of February 1968 to Adorno:

I have given your greetings to Szondi. I don't believe there's anything in these rumours that he's negotiating a professorship here in Jerusalem. I would know about it. People here would certainly be interested in the idea, but

I don't believe that it would be reciprocated. He has come here out of some kind of dark impulse but in a for him wholly uncharacteristic buoyant mood. There is about him however such an air of isolation and not-wanting-to-come-out-of-himself, a tendency to depression and an inability to fully take part in things, which have oppressed those of us who have had much to do with him and struck other people too. It seems that a dreadful, deep-rooted feeling of guilt is erupting within him, precisely through being in contact with a Jewish society, which makes him feel guilty, because he was saved in the famous Kasztner train in 1944, at the expense, he feels, of others. This thought drills into him more than anyone can imagine. It is hard for him to confide in others. With us he only speaks passionately when he gets onto the subject of the goings on with the students in Berlin. Next week I am travelling with him up to Tiberias and will show him a little of the holy places of the Kabbalists. Perhaps something will sink in somewhere. I admit, one could hardly word it more indefinitely than that. In a nutshell, a highly talented and complicated and prodigiously unhappy person. This, between us.

Scholem had put his finger on the wound. In 1965, Szondi, normally exceptionally reticent about his own life and his Jewishness, told the poet Hilde Domin: 'We are all survivors and every one of us is trying to deal with that shame in his own way.' In Jerusalem Szondi collapsed into a deep melancholia. He gave classes in what was then a small department, where Lea Goldberg, Tuvia Schlonsky and Heda Steinberg also taught; he travelled around the country and photographed the Dead Sea; he met Gershon Shaked, Amos Oz and Werner Kraft; he spent a 'Swiss evening' with Friedrich Dürrenmatt and his wife, who were in Jerusalem just then, at the home of Scholem's friends Karl and Kitty Steinschneider; and in April 1968 he finally returned to an unsettled Berlin. A good year later he wrote from there to Scholem:

In the last months I have had to think a great deal about my stay in Israel; only now has everything that I experienced and absorbed with you become again wholly alive. Though it was often difficult for me, it meant a great deal, enough to make Israel a fixed point in my inner geography, without any Zionism (if I can say that). In future it will play an important role in all my reflections as a "self-displaced person". Homesickness is a peculiar thing. You can (re)discover your homeland in three months without realizing it and without accepting it. But that is no subject for a letter.

In January 1970 Lea Goldberg died aged just fifty-eight, and Scholem asked Szondi whether he were prepared to take over her chair. He declined in a long letter, declaring:

Once in Jerusalem you explained why I live in Germany and will probably remain there, in a phrase unsurprising from a man of your insight, but unforgettable nonetheless: you said it is because I have unlearned how to be at home. (I was as little at home in my Budapest childhood as in Zürich and, strictly speaking, in another sense, never was when with my parents.) That is a sickness one could perhaps cure with the drastic treatment of being forced to emigrate, for whatever reason; so much the less can I find the strength to do so of my own free will. Two years ago, when I was in Jerusalem I sensed not only that I was at home but that I could not endure being so. That I could and should change this in myself, I know, but this knowing is not strong enough to break through the resistance inside me – which means as long as I can bear it in Germany. My feelings as I write this last sentence, one week after the arson attack in Munich, I am sure I do not need to tell you.

On 13 February 1970, arsonists had attacked the retirement home of the Jewish community in Munich, killing seven and injuring eight others. Holocaust survivors were among the casualties. The perpetrators were never caught. He did not believe, Scholem replied, that Szondi would end his days in Germany.

In October 1971 Peter Szondi drowned himself in Berlin's Halensee lake. His remains were not found until weeks later. Scholem travelled to Berlin for the memorial service and dedicated his essay on 'Walter Benjamin and his angel' to 'the memory of Peter Szondi, in whose seminar these connections were first aired'. It was published in July 1972, as Suhrkamp Verlag was commemorating what would have been Benjamin's eightieth birthday, and offers a discourse on the figure of the angel in Benjamin, one of the defining figures of thought of the second half of the last century. The discussion starts out from Paul Klee's picture *Angelus Novus*, which Benjamin owned. In this picture, for Benjamin, the utopian aspect of deliverance, of hope on the basis of the past, intersects with noisy futility and despair:

The angel of history must look like this. He has turned his countenance to the past. Where *for us* a chain of events appears, *he* sees a single catastrophe, which heaps ruin unrelentingly on ruin and hurls it at his feet. He would like to pause, to wake the dead and piece together the shattered. But a storm is blowing out of paradise; the wind has caught in his wings and is so strong that the angel can no longer close them. This storm drives him irresistibly into the future, to which his back is turned, while the heap of ruin in front of him grows up into the sky. That which we call progress is *this* storm.

Paul Klee's image of *Angelus Novus* from Benjamin's estate hung for decades in Scholem's study in his house in Rehavia.

'Say, that Jerusalem is': Ilana Shmueli and Paul Celan

When Paul Celan came to Israel at the beginning of October 1969, he met up with Ilana Shmueli. Shmueli, maiden name Lyane Josephine Schindler, was four yours younger than Paul Antschel, who only later took the name Celan and was born, like her, in Czernowitz (in Ukrainian, Chernivtsi) in the 1920s. She had met him in her childhood and again as a young adult in the ghetto that the German soldiers had set up in the city in 1941.

In June 1942 Celan's parents were deported, while for him a hiding place opened up. 'Paul stayed behind, stricken,' Ilana Shmueli remembered. 'He had let his parents go on their own and saved himself. That felt to him like a betrayal. His farewell to his mother was unbearable to him. He could barely speak of it – he found expression for the rupture and pain in his poems. He didn't yet know the ultimate loss that awaited him.' Celan's parents were killed in German camps. The young lovers were torn apart.

Shmueli's parents left Czernowitz in 1944 with their only daughter – the beloved older sister had taken her own life – and managed by onerous pathways to reach Palestine: 'We have arrived! My father is sick and helpless, my mother is confused and helpless and I at twenty years of age am clueless, dependent on others, unrealistic and helpless.' Paul Celan went westwards, via Bucharest to Vienna and ultimately his dreamed-of Paris. Over twenty years later Shmueli met him there, brought together half by chance.

Over one evening in September 1965 the two of them walked about Paris, into the night and through to the early morning, noisily remembering their childhoods and youth as they told each other about their new lives. Celan had become a famous, established poet, with a wife and child in Paris, and yet was still haunted by the past, contesting it, despairing of it. Shmueli had built a family, had a husband and daughter, and had helped introduce social pedagogy to Israel. In her first years she was concerned with the upbringing of young people who had arrived in the country from concentration camps, orphaned, disturbed, devastated. In later years she focused on the integration of young Russian emigrants. After a long period of separation, their love returned.

'I want to show you Jerusalem,' wrote Ilana on a postcard two years later. The city became the emphatic location for their meeting. On 9 October 1969 Celan read his poems at Beit Agron (then the Centre for Journalists, today a cultural centre on the edge of Rehavia). He re-met friends from his youth in Czernowitz: David Seidmann, Hersh Segal, Israel Chalfen – and Ilana Shmueli. She showed him the city on a long tour, from Mount Scopus via the Mount of Olives, the Church of Mary Magdalene and the Church of All Nations at Gethsemane to the Tomb of Absalom. They made their way to the American Colony Hotel in East Jerusalem, in a wide arc towards Bethlehem and Abu Tor, the windmill, David's Tomb, on to the Abbey of the Dormition, past Zion Gate to Jaffa Gate and finally into Café Atara.

'It was the evening of the 9th October. The hall at the new Centre for Journalists in Jerusalem was overflowing with people wanting to experience Celan,' wrote Israel Chalfen in his November 1969 magazine article 'Paul Celan in Jerusalem':

> Not all found seats; some had to listen standing up. The interest in Celan here united widely disparate circles and people. There were people from Bukovina and German Jews, former Austrians and former Czechoslovaks, university professors and poets, artists and teachers, doctors and engineers. And yes even some students from the Hebrew University were in attendance, who probably struggled to understand the German, but knew about Celan – and that is the main thing!

The evening began with speeches from Yehuda Amichai, already then a significant Israeli poet, who was born Ludwig Pfeuffer in Würzburg but had grown up in Israel – 'a Hebrew', our chronicler of the evening calls him – and Manfred Winkler, born 1922 in Czernowitz, who had not been able to emigrate until 1959 but who later wrote poetry and prose in Hebrew. That evening Celan refrained from 'reading out the poems of his great mourning, which had contributed the most to his fame', as his later biographer Chalfen reports. Only with his reading of 'Engführung' ('Stretto'), taking us into a former concentration camp, did he make an exception.

Celan gave readings in Tel Aviv and Haifa, visited Gershom Scholem, met Werner Kraft among others and finally flew back to Paris four days early. He had hoped, Shmueli reported, to find in Israel something of the support and security he needed. And in a certain sense, he did. The great obstacle, however, 'was the conflict of languages'; he felt that he, here in Jerusalem – in Israel – could not and ought not write German, if he wanted to belong to that world. 'That Jerusalem would be a turning point, a caesura in my life – this I knew,' he wrote to his friend.

In December 1969 Shmueli flew to Paris to brave Celan's crises and doubts and raise his hopes. She wrote advising him to focus on small, achievable external tasks – to cling to his 'reeds in the water', as Shmueli calls them. On 12 April 1970 Celan wrote to her: 'Don't be anxious if no post arrives from me for a while – eight or ten days: they've called a postal strike from tomorrow.' She flew once again to Paris, where people were looking for Celan. He had drowned himself in the Seine, probably on 19 April 1970.

Over thirty years later, Shmueli worked a summer long preparing her correspondence with Celan for publication, a unique document of love and trust, with precise particulars and dazzling images of places and faces. The two often exchanged poems like letters. Shmueli wrote her memories of him under a line from his poetry – 'Say, that Jerusalem is' – and she herself composed poems about the woods and the seasons of their origins, the fresh snowfall, 'white as never again', the 'lilacs of back then, the dreams in the walnut trees, small green-brown fingers on rough bark – can all this still be named?'

Shmueli belonged to 'Lyris', the German-speaking circle of poets that had formed in Jerusalem, with Manfred Winkler, Annemarie Königsberger, Magali Zibaso and others. The group absorbed a great deal from the polyglot world of Czernowitz, capital city of lyric poetry, capital city of the incommensurable. She won the Theodor Kramer Prize and on 28 May 2009 she presented her poetry at what was then the Literature Workshop and is today the House for Poetry in Berlin. Her face, as ever, was as if bathed in light by the beacons of her punctuation, the initial scepticism of her question marks, which grow into exclamation marks, and the many dashes, without a concluding full stop. On 11 November 2011 Ilana Shmueli died in Jerusalem. Some years before, she had noted down one last question: 'In which language will death come to me?'

Rehavia Revisited

Rehavia is laid out as a grid, but its history cannot be told symmetrically or in straight lines. It is patterned like a zig-zag, like broken threads which run in parallel or at some point in the future are knotted back together. There are 'native' residents of long standing and temporary visitors. There are chance encounters, romantic or less romantic, marriages and divorces, neighbourliness both simple and complicated, as well as periods of inevitable evolution or sudden change, friendships and hostilities.

In a city neighbourhood you must always grant a large role to chance. People are pleased to talk about the area where they live, but only rarely do they understand it – and still less themselves within it – as the product of historical evolution. The city neighbourhood is not a well-developed historical category. As a result only a very few of the testimonies, letters and diaries of residents actually turn their attention to their neighbourhood as such. With Rehavia it is no different. Only with the hindsight of history does the importance of an area as context become visible, from the formation of the neighbourhood, through periods of continuity and evolution, until it has been radically transformed. Literary texts, be they by Else Lasker-Schüler, S.Y. Agnon or Amos Oz, offer the most penetrating descriptions of it.

The guests in Café Atara at the beginning of the book were brought together not by chance but by my design, to show a constellation: the two gatekeepers, Gershom Scholem and Werner Kraft, who both lived in Rehavia for decades; Martin Buber, resident of Talbiya but honorary citizen of Rehavia; Mascha Kaléko, on the last stop of her long emigration; Hannah Arendt, the visitor; and Yehuda Amichai and Lea Goldberg, the writers. The time period spans the 1920s up to the 1960s, as the character of the area changes utterly.

In 1966 the magazine *Neue Sammlung* published an essay by the Berlin theologian and educator Rudolf Lennert entitled 'On the Life of the German Language in Jerusalem', about the survival of German-language poetry by Kraft, Lasker-Schüler, Ernst Simon and Ludwig Strauß. It offers something like a stock-taking of German in Jerusalem at that time. It's striking that its author writes about the past and the present of German in Jerusalem, but not its future. True, Kraft and Scholem were by then around seventy years old, and Lennert could not have foreseen that both had still quite a few productive years ahead of them. But Lennert's essay describes the beginning of the end of Rehavia as a German-Jewish neighbourhood – not an abrupt end, but a long, gradual transformation. In the same issue, Shmuel Hugo Bergmann writes about Buber, who had died the previous year and had been the central figure of the German-Jewish 'dialogue' of the preceding years, and Ernst Simon discusses 'Tradition and Future in Israel', based on a lecture he gave at the Volkshochschule ('Adult Education College') in Hanover. The organiser of that event had added the subtitle 'Israelis or Jews?' and in doing so was asking about the decisive change. For the next generation, the children of the emigrants, and still more for their grandchildren, German-Jewish Rehavia was becoming Israeli Rehavia. The relationship between Germans and Jews, as discussed at the 1966 Jewish World Congress in Brussels, was gaining a new emphasis. Now the question was also, or indeed directly, about the relationship of Germans and Israelis.

In spaces we read time and can at least to some degree distinguish the decades: the founding of Rehavia by Richard Kauffmann and Lotte Cohn was indebted to the idea of the garden city, but other energies flowed into its creation as well. The artists' colonies of the early years of the twentieth century had lent it wings: you might almost take Lasker-Schüler's image of Rehavia's houses literally, with wings growing on their backs to carry them up to heaven, because they did descend from the heaven of ideas. Lasker-Schüler had been – albeit briefly – a member of the Neue Gemeinschaft, an anarchist-communist commune at Schlachtensee in Berlin. In Rehavia she rediscovered its feeling of community, of participation and exchange, its manageable number of residents and guests, and its reverence for literature, painting and art. With her 'Kraal' she passed those values on. That this idealistic impetus did not later withstand the impact of reality does not diminish the force of its beginning. Cohn and Scholem convey a vivid picture of Rehavia at its beginning in the 1920s and early 1930s.

The bright image of an energetic start grows darker. By the time Lasker-Schüler first came to Jerusalem in 1934 the persecution of Germany's Jews was already underway and getting worse; more and more immigrants were fleeing to Palestine. The British authorities denied many the coveted certificate. In

1939, a few months before the outbreak of the Second World War, the poet travelled to Jerusalem for the third time. In her letters you can read how the news of the persecution and murder of Europe's Jews had already forced its way into Jerusalem and all of Palestine.

Even in its beginnings Rehavia was no idyll. But the experience of the millionfold murder of relatives, friends, companions in fate – an event for which for a long time there was no word – changed the life of the German-Jewish neighbourhood forever. The journalist Asher Beilin described the nameless despairing on the streets of Rehavia. No one asked after them or paid attention to them. He was writing in 1941, just as the first deportation trains were rolling away to the east from platform 17 at Berlin's Grunewald station. And still the British Mandatory Power blocked the immigration of Jewish refugees. After the end of the Second World War, ships like the *Exodus*, waiting off the country's coast and filled with survivors from the concentration camps, were forced to turn back.

Rehavia under siege gives an impression of how embattled the city of Jerusalem was when David Ben-Gurion declared Israel's independence in Tel Aviv in May 1948.

Amos Oz mentions his move to Rehavia in 1953 only in parenthesis: '(By now we were living in the new flat, at 28 Ben Maimon [Boulevard], in Rehavia, the area of Jerusalem where [my father] had longed to live for years.)' But when you move into your dream, your dream ends. Oz describes how, a year after his mother's death, he and his father – who remarried in the meantime – were still talking only about everyday necessities. Oz hardly goes any more to his school, the Hebrew Gymnasium. Eventually, a year later, he moves into the Hulda kibbutz.

In his works, however, Oz returns to Jerusalem again and again, in his novel *My Michael* of 1965 and fifty years later with *Judas*, the story of a dreamy young student, Shmuel Ash, who in the winter of 1959 and 1960 takes a room in a secret-filled house in Jerusalem's Sha'arei Hesed neighbourhood. Day after day he listens to an old man, Gershom Wald, telling him about his son, Micha, who fell in the 'War of Independence', inspired by Zionist ideals, which his father had conveyed to him and which now give way to a raven-black scepticism. He tells of his son's deceased father-in-law, Shealtiel Abravanel (an echo of Abarbanel), who turned against his former comrade David Ben-Gurion to advocate a solution to the Arab–Israeli conflict. Was Abravanel right after all? And how ought we to assess his betrayal and the betrayer? In the same house lives Micha's widow, Atalia Abravanel, with whom the student, twenty years her junior, falls in love. Oz's *Judas* is set in a neighbouring area, but in the combination of its names, locations and motifs we can recognise something of Rehavia.

The 1950s in Rehavia are characterised by separation and abandonment. In November 1958 Siegmund Kaznelson published in Jerusalem *Jewish Fate in German Poetry*, subtitled *A Definitive Anthology*. Kaznelson had directed the Jüdischer Verlag ('Jewish Publishing House') in Berlin in the 1920s, and in 1934 brought out his great compendium *Jews in German Culture*, which the Nazi government banned as soon as it appeared. It was eventually republished in 1959 by the Jüdischer Verlag, the same place of publication as the poems: two collections attesting to Jewish culture in Germany, selected and edited in Jerusalem. Kaznelson designated his anthology 'definitive', 'not only because it concludes a thousand-year-long period of history but because, by any reasonable assessment, German-language poetry on Jewish subjects is coming to an end with our or perhaps the next generation.' Many understood the 1955 foundation of the Leo Baeck Institute for Research into the History of the Jews from Germany, with its centres in Jerusalem, New York and London, as a similar end point, for the gathering and sifting of a history that had concluded.

Kaznelson had tentatively asked, nevertheless, whether the old prophecy might still hold: 'A remnant will return.' Just five years later another anthology appeared, *Shalom: Stories from Israel*, which familiarised German readers with authors, from Agnon to Yishar, whom they barely knew. This first collection was edited by Eva Rottenberg, a young Swiss, originally from Budapest, who was studying in Jerusalem. Later, by now Eva Koralnik, she went on to run a literary agency in Zürich with Ruth Liepman and Ruth Weibel, which represents to this day virtually every significant Israeli author and a great many Jewish authors and their work.

On 14 October 1963, when the Cologne City Museum opened 'Monumenta Judaica', the first large exhibition of its kind in Germany, on '2,000 years of Jewish history and culture on the Rhine', Theodor Schieder, the Rector of Cologne University and chair of the academic committee for the exhibition, solemnly announced that the university was establishing a professorship and an institute for Jewish Studies, which would bear the name of Martin Buber. He recalled the victims of 'atrocious terror' – to which he had contributed, as only became known decades later, through his work as a Nazi historian. Schieder and his colleagues in Cologne invited guests from Jerusalem for the supporting programme: Ernst Simon spoke in March 1964 on behalf of Buber, Scholem lectured on Jewish mysticism, and Moshe Ya'akov Ben-Gavriêl read from his work. Rehavia as guest in Cologne – something that would have been barely imaginable in previous years, leaving aside that unique, early guest in Germany, Martin Buber.

Noam Zadoff has shown the stages by which Scholem, after years of resistance, made his way from Jerusalem to Berlin – which, in this case, means to Germany. In 1963 his first volume of *Judaica* appeared from Suhrkamp Verlag. Siegfried Unseld signed the author, whose works had appeared until then in German from Rhein Verlag in Switzerland. The two became friends.

Scholem also made a connection with Jürgen Habermas, in whom he recognised a proponent of critical theory in a, so to speak, academically disciplined form. Their relationship shared some features with his friendship with George Lichtheim, to whom Scholem wrote in November 1967:

I don't know if you have ever yet seen Jürgen Habermas, whom you mentioned, in person. He is of a peculiar appearance; that is to say, implausible as it seems, a goyish edition of the physiognomy of Walter Benjamin. It's almost enough to give one occult ideas.

Many years later Habermas wrote in *Münchner Beiträgen zur Jüdischen Geschichte und Kultur* ('Munich Articles on Jewish History and Culture'):

We travelled with Siegfried Unseld to the celebration of Scholem's 80th birthday. Scholem enjoyed the reception at the residence of the German ambassador Schütz, formerly the governing mayor of Berlin. The highpoint was a reading by the man we were celebrating. Scholem read from his just published autobiography *From Berlin to Jerusalem*. A large audience of predominantly older age groups had assembled in the concert hall. They evidently had no difficulty following the sharply articulated sentences of this master of German prose. As a Rhinelander, I was struck by how a murmur of recognition ran through the auditorium at every Berlin street name. [...] In 1978 in Tel Aviv, near to a city district designed by Bauhaus architects, you could sense the historic nature of the moment: that here, as if for the last time, a generation of Yekkes had gathered itself at the feet of a monumental figure, who had arisen from their midst.

At the end of his life Scholem returned from Rehavia, the 'Grunewald of the East', one last time, with extensive book plans in his luggage, to be a fellow at the Institute for Advanced Study which had opened in Berlin – in Grunewald.

Rehavia, the city of books, is taking on a new form. And in that similar place, in Berlin's Grunewald, Fania Oz-Salzberger, historian and daughter of Amos Oz, writes about the journeys, the lives, the search for traces of mostly young Israelis in Berlin.

Acknowledgements

I gratefully recall my many conversations about Rehavia and its inhabitants with Kitty Steinschneider (1905–2002) – 'the charming Miss Marx', as Betty Scholem called her in 1926.

Itta Shedletzky opened the gates of Rehavia for me and made a great many encounters and acquaintances possible.

Thank you to Amnon Ramon from Yad Ben-Zvi in Jerusalem for his suggestions and insights into the history of the city over the course of my work. I am indebted to Caroline Jessen (Marbach am Neckar) for valuable bibliographical references, including on Franziska Baruch. Stefan Litt, the German memory at the National Library in Jerusalem, enabled me to make discoveries of previously unpublished sources in their archive. Caroline Jessen and Stefan Litt both checked sections of my manuscript. My sincere thanks to them both.

My remarks on the religious communities in Rehavia have their essential origin in Christian Kraft's book on the subject. I am indebted to David Kroyanker for the insights I gained into Jerusalem's architecture in a conversation with him.

Thank you to Heinrich von Berenberg for his faith in me, to Ulla Mothes for her editing and to Eva-Maria Thimme for proofreading.

I am grateful to Elisheva Bard for her Hebrew lessons and

to Eldad Stobetzky for the translation of particular texts. For tips and suggestions, thank you to Dominique Bourel, Cilly Kugelmann, Giddon Ticotsky, Alisa Eschad, Meira Meisler, Carney and Tal Griffit, Itay Friedman, the late Raimund Fellinger, Thomas Meyer, Norbert Kron and Jutta Rosenkranz.

For their encouragement and support I remain thankful to Andreas Kossert, Amir Eshel, Astrid Schmetterling and especially Eva Koralnik and Marc Koralnik.

For the impetus and for his thoughtfulness and companionship, I thank Matthias Dotschko.

I thank Barbara Schwepcke and Harry Hall of Haus Publishing very much for publishing this English-language edition and I thank Stephen Brown for his excellent translation.

Bibliography

Quotations have not been individually referenced but may be tracked down in the following bibliography. English translations are listed where they exist.

Theodor W. Adorno / Gershom Scholem, *Correspondence: 1939–1969*. Edited by Asaf Angermann. From the German by Sebastian Truskolaski and Paula Schwebel. Polity Press, Cambridge, 2020

S.Y. Agnon, *Shira*. From the Hebrew by Zeva Shapiro. Toby Press, New Milford, 2013

Hannah Arendt / Gershom Scholem, *The Correspondence of Hannah Arendt and Gershom Scholem*. Edited by Marie Luise Knott. From the German by Anthony David. University of Chicago Press, Chicago and London, 2017

Shalom Ben-Chorin, *Ich lebe in Jerusalem. Ein Bekenntnis zu Geschichte und Gegenwart* ['I Live in Jerusalem: A Commitment to History and the Present']. Gerlingen, Bleicher Verlag, 1979

Moshe Ya'akov Ben-Gavriêl, *Die Gedichte* ['Poems']. Rothenburg ob der Tauber, Verlag J.P. Peter, 1964

–: *Jerusalem wird verkauft oder Gold auf der Straße. Ein Tatsachenroman* ['Jerusalem is For Sale, or Gold in

the Streets. A Documentary Novel']. Edited with an
afterword by Sebastian Schirrmeister. Wuppertal, Arco
Verlag, 2016

Walter Benjamin, *The Correspondence of Walter Benjamin:
1910–1940*. Edited and annotated by Gershom Scholem
and Theodor W. Adorno. From the German by Manfred
R. Jacobson and Evelyn M. Jacobson. University of
Chicago Press, Chicago and London, 1994

Walter Benjamin / Gershom Scholem, *The Correspondence of
Walter Benjamin and Gershom Scholem, 1932–1940*. Edited
by Gershom Scholem. From the German by Gary Smith
and André Lefevre. Schocken Books, New York, 1989

Shmuel Hugo Bergmann, *Tagebücher und Briefe*
['Diaries and Letters']. Two Volumes. Edited by
Miriam Sambursky. With an Introduction by Nathan
Rotenstreich. Königstein im Taunus, Jüdischer Verlag bei
Athenäum, 1985

David Biale, *Gershom Scholem: Kabbalah and Counter-
History*. Harvard University Press, Cambridge Mass., (2nd
ed.) 1982

Dominique Bourel, 'Le village "yekke": capitale du judaisme
allemand' ['The "yekke" Village: Capital of German
Judaism']. In *L'Histoire*. 7–8, 2013. Nr. 378.

–: *Martin Buber: Sentinelle de l'humanité* [Martin Buber:
Sentinel of Humanity]. Editions Albin Michel, Paris, 2015

Michael Brenner, *In Search of Israel: The History of an Idea*.
Princeton University Press, Princeton, 2018

Edna Brocke, 'Selbst denken macht einsam. Über "Hannah
Arendt"' ['Thinking for yourself makes you lonely: On

"Hannah Arendt'"]. In *Frankfurter Allgemeine Zeitung*, 14 January 2013

Martin Buber, *Briefwechsel aus sieben Jahrzehnten* ['Correspondence from Seven Decades']. Three volumes. Edited and introduced by Grete Schaeder in consultation with Ernst Simon and in collaboration with Rafael Buber, Margot Cohn and Gabriel Stern. Verlag Lambert Schneider, Heidelberg, 1972–1975.

–: *The Letters of Martin Buber: A Life of Dialogue* (Selected and edited translation of *Briefwechsel aus sieben Jahrzehnten*). Edited by Nahum N. Glatzer and Paul Mendes-Flohr. From the German by Richard and Clara Winston and Harry Zohn. Schocken Books, New York, 1991

Elias Canetti, *The Play of the Eyes*. From the German by Ralph Manheim. Farrar Straus & Giroux, New York, 1986 / Granta, London, 2011

Paul Celan / Ilana Shmueli, *The Correspondence of Paul Celan and Ilana Shmueli*. Edited by Ilana Shmueli and Thomas Sparr. From the German by Susan H. Gillespie. Sheep Meadow Press, Riverdale-on-Hudson, New York, 2010

Dan Diner, *Rituelle Distanz: Israels deutsche Frage* ['Ritual Distance: Israel's German Question']. Deutsche Verlags-Anstalt, Munich, 2015

Alisa Eshad, *Quatsch mit Soße* (documentary film), Association of Israelis of Central European Origin, 2013. Available on YouTube: https://www.youtube.com/ watch?v=h9dn6J8x_5U. Accessed 21 October 2020.

Reuven Gafni, *Mikdash me'at: Batei Knesset muchrim*

ve-nistarim be-Yerushalayim ['A Little Sanctuary: Familiar
and Hidden Synagogues in Jerusalem']. Yad Ben-Zvi
Press, Jerusalem, 2004

Lea Goldberg, *Pegishah im Meshorer. Al Avraham
Ben-Yitzhak* ['Encounter with a Poet: On Avraham Ben-
Yitzhak']. Ha-Kibbutz Ha-Me'uhad and Sifriyat Poalim,
Tel Aviv, 2009

–: *Selected Poetry and Drama.* Poetry selected, translated and
introduced by Rachel Tzvia Back. Drama translated by
T. Carmi. Toby Press, New Milford, Connecticut and
London, 2005

–: 'Begegnung mit einem Dichter'. In German, from the
Hebrew by Markus Lemke. In *Naharaim. Zeitschrift für
deutsch-jüdische Literatur und Kulturgeschichte* ['Naharaim:
Journal of German-Jewish Literature and Cultural
History']. Edited by Yfaat Weiss. 7, 2013, Nr. 1 / 2, pp.
1–50

Erich Gottgetreu, *Die 37. Belagerung von Jerusalem. Ein
Tagebuch aus dem Frühjahr 1948* ['The 37th Siege of
Jerusalem: A Diary of Spring 1948']. Rubin Mass,
Jerusalem, 1985

Gad Granach, *Where is Home? Stories from the Life of a
German-Jewish Émigré.* From the German by David
Edward Lane. Atara Press, Los Angeles, 2009

Raphael Gross, 'The Eichmann Trial'. In *Encyclopedia of
Jewish History and Culture.* Edited by Dan Diner. Volume
2. Brill, Leiden, 2019

Jürgen Habermas, 'Begegnungen mit Gershom Scholem'
['Encounters with Gershom Scholem']. In *Münchner*

Beiträge zur Jüdischen Geschichte und Kultur. 2007, Nr. 2, pp. 9–18.

Yehudah Haezrahi, *Ir, even ve-shamayim* ['City of Stone and Sky']. Israeli Defence Ministry Publishing, (2nd ed.) 1972

Niels Hansen, *Aus dem Schatten der Katastrophe. Die deutsch-israelischen Beziehungen in der Ära Konrad Adenauer and David Ben-Gurion* ['Out of the Shadow of Catastrophe: German-Israeli Relations in the Era of Konrad Adenauer and David Ben-Gurion']. Droste, Düsseldorf, 2002

Georg Herlitz, *Mein Weg nach Jerusalem. Erinnerungen eines zionistischen Beamten* ['My Way to Jerusalem: Memoirs of a Zionist Official']. Rubin Mass, Jerusalem, 1964

Jenny Hestermann, *Inszenierte Versöhnung. Reisediplomatie und die deutsch-israelischen Beziehungen von 1957 bis 1984* ['Staging Atonement: Shuttle Diplomacy and German-Israeli Relations from 1957 to 1984']. Campus Verlag, Frankfurt am Main, 2016

Caroline Jessen, *Kanon im Exil. Lektüren deutsch-jüdischer Emigranten in Palästina/Israel* ['A Canon in Exile: The Reading of German-Jewish Émigrés in Palestine / Israel']. Wallstein Verlag, Göttingen, 2019

Anna Maria Jokl, *Essenzen* ['Essences']. Jüdischer Verlag im Suhrkamp Verlag, Frankfurt am Main, 1993

–: *Aus sechs Leben* ['Of Six Lives']. Edited and with an afterword by Jennifer Tharr. With an essay by Itta Shedletzky. Jüdischer Verlag im Suhrkamp Verlag, Berlin, 2011

Hans Jonas, *Memoirs.* Edited and annotated by Christian Wiese. From the German by Krishna Winston and

Ammon Allred. Brandeis University Press, Lebanon, New Hampshire, 2008

Wolf Kaiser, *Palästina – Erez Israel. Deutschsprachige Reisebeschreibungen jüdischer Autoren von den Jahrhundertwende bis zum Zweiten Weltkrieg* ['Palestine – Eretz Israel: German-language Travelogues by Jewish Authors from the Turn of the Century to the Second World War']. Georg Olms Verlag, Hildesheim et al., 1992

Mascha Kaléko, *In Exile: Poems by Hilde Domin*, Mascha Kaléko, Hans Sahl. From the German by Ruth Ingram. Highgate Poets, Hertford, 2011

–: *Sämtliche Werke und Briefe* ['Complete Works and Letters']. Edited by Jutta Rosenkranz. dtv, Munich, 2012.

–: *Mascha: The Poems of Mascha Kaléko*. From the German by Andreas Nolte. Fomite Press, Burlington, Vermont, (2nd ed.) 2017

Siegmund Kaznelson ed., *Jüdisches Schicksal in deutschen Gedichten. Eine abschließende Anthologie* ['Jewish Fate in German Poetry: A Definitive Anthology']. Jüdischer Verlag, Berlin, 1959

Christian Kraft, *Aschkenas in Jerusalem. Die religiösen Institutionen der Einwanderer aus Deutschland im Jerusalemer Stadtviertel Rechavia (1933–2004) – Transfer und Transformation* ['Ashkenazi in Jerusalem: The Religious Institutions of German Immigrants in the Jerusalem District Rehavia (1933–2004) – Transfer and Transformation']. Vandenhoeck & Ruprecht, Göttingen, 2014

Werner Kraft, *Gespräche mit Martin Buber* ['Conversations with Martin Buber']. Kösel Verlag, Munich, 1966

Werner Kraft / Wilhelm Lehmann, *Briefwechsel 1931–1968* ['Correspondence 1931–1968']. Edited by Ricarda Dick. Wallstein Verlag, Göttingen, 2008

David Kroyanker, *Jerusalem Architecture*. Introduction by Teddy Kollek. Tauris Parke, London, 1994 / Vendome Press, London, 2003

–: 'Rechavia – das "Jeckenland" von Jerusalem' ['Rehavia – Jerusalem's "Yekkeland"']. In *Zweimal Heimat. Die Jeckes zwischen Mitteleuropa und Nahost* ['Two Homelands: The Yekkes between Central Europe and the Middle East']. Edited by Moshe Zimmermann and Yotam Hatam. Beerenverlag, Frankfurt am Main, 2003, pp. 260–266

–: 'The Ghosts of Rehavia's Zeitgeist'. In *Haaretz*, 30 April 2004. Available online: www.haaretz.com/1.4828323. Accessed 19 October 2020.

–: *MiGermania lemoledet chadasha. Gustav ve-Edith Kroyanker. Chronika shel sichron mishpachati* ['From Germany to a New Homeland: Gustav and Edith Kroyanker. A Chronicle of the Memories in My Family']. Privately printed, 2013

Walter Laqueur, *Dying for Jerusalem: The Past, Present and Future of the Holiest City*. Sourcebooks, Napierville, Illinois, 2006

Else Lasker-Schüler, *Werke und Briefe* ['Works and Letters']. Critical edition. Edited by Andreas B. Kilcher, Norbert Oellers, Heinz Röllecke and Itta Shedletzky. Jüdischer Verlag im Surhkamp Verlag, Frankfurt am Main, 1996 onwards

–: *And the Bridge is Love: Memories of a Lifetime*. In

collaboration with E.B. Ashton. Harcourt Brace, New
York, 1958
–: *My Blue Piano*. From the German by Brooks Haxton.
Syracuse University Press, Syracuse, New York, 2015
Alma Mahler Werfel, *Mein Leben* ['My Life']. S. Fischer
Verlag, Frankfurt am Main, 1963
Thomas Mann, 'Lübeck as a Way of Life and Thought',
included with *Buddenbrooks*. From the German by H.T.
Lowe-Porter. Alfred A. Knopf, New York, 1983
Simon Sebag Montefiore, *Jerusalem: the Biography*.
Weidenfeld & Nicolson, London, 2011
Ulrich Ott ed., 'Werner Kraft (1896–1991)'. Issue of
Marbacher Magazin 75 / 1996. Additional editing by
Jörg Drews. Editorial team: Friedrich Pfäfflin. Deutsche
Schillergesellschaft, Marbach am Neckar, 1996
Amos Oz, *A Tale of Love and Darkness*. From the Hebrew by
Nicholas de Lange. Chatto & Windus, London, 2004
Fania Oz-Salzberger, *Israelis in Berlin*. In German, from the
Hebrew by Mirjam Pressler. Suhrkamp Verlag, Frankfurt
am Main, 2004
Amnon Ramon, *"Doktor mul doktor gar". Shechuna Rehavia
be-Yerushalayim* ['"Doctor Dwells Opposite Doctor":
Jerusalem's Rehavia District']. Yad Ben-Zvi Press,
Jerusalem, (3rd ed.) 2006
Eva Rottenberg ed., *Schalom. Erzählungen aus Israel*
['Shalom: Stories from Israel']. Foreword by Heinrich
Böll. Diogenes Verlag, Zürich, 1964
Tuvia Rübner, *Ein langes kurzes Leben. Von Pressburg
nach Merchavia* ['A long, short life: From Pressburg to

Merhavia']. Enlarged and illustrated edition. Rimbaud
Verlag, Aachen, 2014

Arthur Ruppin, *Briefe, Tagebücher, Erinnerungen* ['Letters,
Diaries, Memoirs']. Edited by Shlomo Krolik. Jüdischer
Verlag bei Athenäum, Königstein im Taunus, 1985

Shmuel Sambursky, *Nicht-imaginäre Porträts. Jerusalem
und Tel Aviv* ['Un-imaginary Portraits: Jerusalem and Tel
Aviv']. Haaretz Press Ltd, 1960

Betty Scholem / Gershom Scholem, *Mutter und Sohn im
Briefwechsel 1917–1946* ['Letters of a Mother and Son,
1917–1946']. Edited by Itta Shedletzky in collaboration
with Thomas Sparr. Verlag C.H. Beck, Munich, 1989

Gershom Scholem, 'At the Completion of Buber's
Translation of the Bible'. In *The Messianic Idea in Judaism
(and other essays on Jewish Spirituality)*. From the German
by Michael A. Meyer and Hillel Halkin. Schocken Books,
New York, 1971

–: 'Walter Benjamin und sein Engel' ['Walter Benjamin
and his Angel']. In *Zur Aktualität Walter Benjamins* ['On
the Timeliness of Walter Benjamin']. Edited by Siegfried
Unseld. Suhrkamp Verlag, Frankfurt am Main, 1972, pp.
87–138

–: *Briefe I. 1914–1947* ['Letters I: 1914–1947']. Edited by Itta
Shedletzky. Verlag C.H. Beck, Munich, 1994

–: *Briefe II. 1948–1970* ['Letters II: 1948–1970']. Edited by
Thomas Sparr. Verlag C.H. Beck, Munich, 1995

–: *Briefe III. 1971–1982* ['Letters III: 1971–1982']. Edited by
Itta Shedletzky. Verlag C.H. Beck, Munich, 1995

–: *Gershom Scholem: A Life in Letters, 1914–1982*. Edited and

translated by Anthony David Skinner. Harvard University
Press, Cambridge, Mass., 2002

–: *Walter Benjamin: The Story of a Friendship*. From the
German by Harry Zohn. New York Review Books, New
York, 2003

–: *Von Berlin nach Jerusalem. Jugenderinnerungen* ['From
Berlin to Jerusalem: Memories of My Youth']. From the
Hebrew by Michael Brocke and Andrea Schatz. Jüdischer
Verlag im Suhrkamp Verlag, Frankfurt am Main, 1994

–: *From Berlin to Jerusalem: Memories of My Youth*. From the
German by Harry Zohn. Foreword by Moshe Idel. Paul
Dry Books, Philadelphia, 2012 (This translation is of the
original German edition, published in 1977. Scholem
substantially enlarged his memoir for the Hebrew edition
of 1982, translated into German by Brocke and Schatz,
above.)

–: *Sabbatai Ṣevi: The Mystical Messiah, 1626–1676*. From the
Hebrew by R.J. Zwi Werblowsky. New edition with an
introduction by Yaacob Dweck. Princeton University
Press, Princeton, 2016

Ilana Shmueli, *Sag, dass Jerusalem ist. Über Paul Celan,
Oktober 1969–April 1970* ['Say, that Jerusalem is: On
Paul Celan, October 1969 to April 1970']. Edition Isele,
Eggingen, 2000

Ines Sonder, *Lotte Cohn. Baumeisterin des Landes Israel. Eine
Biographie* ['Lotte Cohn, Woman Master Architect of
the Land of Israel: A Biography']. Jüdischer Verlag im
Suhrkamp Verlag, Frankfurt am Main, 2010

Thomas Sparr, 'Das reizende Fräulein Marx. Zum Tode
von Kitty Steinschneider in Jerusalem' ['The charming

Miss Marx: On the Death of Kitty Steinschneider in
Jerusalem']. In *Frankfurter Rundschau*, 21 November 2002
Ludwig Strauß, *Land Israel. Gedichte* ['Land of Israel:
Poems']. Edited by Hans Otto Horch. Rimbaud Verlag,
Aachen, 1991
—: *Gesammelte Werke in vier Bänden* ['Collected Works in
Four Volumes']. Edited by Tuvia Rübner and Hans Otto
Horch. Wallstein Verlag, Göttingen, 1998
Peter Szondi, *Briefe* ['Letters']. Edited by Christoph König
and Thomas Sparr. Suhrkamp Verlag, Frankfurt am Main,
1993
Gabriele Tergit, *Im Schnellzug nach Haifa* ['On the Express
to Haifa']. With photos from the archive of Abraham
Pisarek. Edited by Jens Brüning and with an afterword by
Joachim Schlör. Transit Verlag, Berlin, 1996
Yfaat Weiss, *Lea Goldberg. Lehrjahre in Deutschland
1930–1933* ['Lea Goldberg: Apprentice Years in Germany,
1930–1933']. From the Hebrew by Liliane Meilinger.
Verlag Vandenhoeck & Ruprecht, Göttingen, 2010
Ernst-Peter Wieckenberg, 'Wiederfinden. Über eine
Anthologie von Werner Kraft' ['Rediscovery: On an
Anthology by Werner Kraft']. In *Münchner Beiträge zur
Jüdischen Geschichte und Kultur* 2009, Nr. 2, pp. 81–97
Wiederfinden. Deutsche Poesie und Prosa ['Rediscovery:
German Poetry and Prose']. A selection by Werner Kraft.
Verlag Lambert Schneider, Heidelberg, 1954
Noam Zadoff, *Gershom Scholem: From Berlin to Jerusalem
and Back: An Intellectual Biography*. From the German by
Jeffrey Green. Brandeis University Press, Lebanon, New
Hampshire, 2018

Hermann Zondek, *Auf festem Fusse. Erinnerungen eines jüdischen Klinikers* ['On a Firm Footing: Memoirs of a Jewish Clinician']. Deutsche Verlagsanstalt, Stuttgart, 1973

Arnold Zweig, *De Vriendt Kehrt Heim* ['De Vriendt Goes Home']. Aufbau Verlag, Berlin, 1996

Index

167, 182
Szondi, Peter 170–5

T
Talmud 51, 69, 75–6, 96
Tanakh 51
Tel Aviv xi–xii, 11, 14, 32–4,
48, 59, 88, 130, 132, 144–5,
152, 155, 162, 165, 169, 179,
184, 188
Tergit, Gabriele 2–4, 36–8,
77
Torah 69, 70–1, 73, 75–6

V
Villa Aghion 27
Vinaver, Chemjo 21,
159–60, 165
von Mildenstein, Leopold
57–60

W
Weimar Republic ix, 2–3,
30, 116, 125, 136

Werfel, Franz 51–4
Werfel-Mahler, Alma *see*
Mahler, Alma

Y
Yad Vashem 169
Yekke ix–x, 16–7, 39, 43,
48–51, 61, 78–9, 83–4, 188
yekkish *see* Yekke
Yiddish 66–8, 111, 131
Yishuv 43, 65, 100, 102
Yom Kippur 5, 8, 77, 88

Z
Zion Square 14
Zionism x, xii, 23, 30, 32,
35–7, 39, 43, 46, 48–9, 51,
55, 57, 59–63, 71, 81, 88–9,
103–5, 110, 114–5, 140, 150,
155, 174, 185